The Authentic
Air Fryer
Recipes Cookbook UK

Amazing and Easy-to-Follow Metric Unit Air Fryer

Recipes Edited Exclusively for the UK

Poppy Power

Table of Contents

1	Introduction
2	Fundamental of Air Frying
9	4-Week Meal Plan
11	Chapter 1 Breakfast Recipes

Chocolate Chip Muffins 11
Super-Filling Calzones 11
Vanilla Cinnamon Rolls 12
Cute Bagels 12
Simple Muffins 13
Ham Eggs 13
Chopped Blueberry Muffins 13
Cheese Pepper Eggs 14
Tomato Egg White Cups 14
Cheddar Spinach Omelet 14
Cheese Soufflés 15
Fluffy Bacon Quiche 15
Vanilla Pancakes 15
Sausage Meatballs 16
Turkey Burgers 16
Tasty Sausage-Crusted Egg Cups 16
Jalapeño & Bacon Pizza 17
Savory Egg Pizza 17
Cinnamon Pecan Granola 17
Fruit Muffins 18
Quinoa Quiche 18
French Whole-Grain Toast 19
Oat Bowls 19
Yummy Jalapeño Egg Cups 19
Homemade Hash Browns 20
Tofu Scramble Brunch 20
Special Patties 21
Power Tarts 21
Onion Avocado Bagels 22
Curry Samosa Rolls 22
Glazed Apple Fritters 23
Apple-Cinnamon Cookies 23
Golden Pancake 24
Glory Muffins 24

| 25 | Chapter 2 Vegetable and Sides Recipes |

Broccoli Salad 25
Crispy Tofu & Sweet Potato 25
Vegan Sandwiches 26
Cheese Bean Taquitos 26
Barbecue Pulled Jackfruit 26
Marinated Tofu Cubes 27

Chili Dogs 27
Stuffed Potatoes with Dressing 28
Broccoli Salad 28
Homemade Giant Nachos 29
Potato-Stuffed Peppers 29
Avocado Tacos 30
Cauliflower Steak 30
Lemon Aubergine Dip 31
Mini Mushroom-Onion Pizzas 31
Breaded White Mushrooms 32
Quinoa Patties 32
Cheese Vegetarian Lasagna 33
Pineapple Salsa 33
Avocado Rice Bowls 34
Cheese Courgette Boats 34
Vegetable Quesadilla 35
Stuffed Aubergine 35
Spinach & Artichoke Casserole 36
Cheese Zoodle 36
Roasted Lemon Cauliflower 37
Cauliflower Pizza Crust 37
Mini Portobello Pizzas 38
Veggie Bowl 38

| 39 | Chapter 3 Starter and Snack Recipes |

Courgette Sticks 39
Simple Courgette 39
Tamari Aubergine 40
Glazed Carrots 40
Fried Green Tomatoes 41
Garlic Tortilla Chips 41
Low-Fat Buffalo Cauliflower 42
Onion Rings 43
Garlic Russet Potatoes 43
Roasted Shishito Peppers 44
"Samosas" with Coriander Chutney 44
Kale Chips 45
Pakoras 45
Simple French Fries 46
French Fries with Shallots 46
Berbere-Spiced Potato Fries 47
Glazed Brussels Sprouts 47
Indian Okra 48
Spring Rolls 48
Fast-Cooked Courgette Rolls 49
Easy-to-Cook Asparagus 49
Sweet Potato Chips 49
Parmesan Courgette Chips 50
Seasoned Sweet Potato Wedges 50
Savoury Potato Wedges 50

51 ▶ Chapter 4 Poultry Recipes

Lemon-Pepper Chicken Thighs	51
Fried Turkey Wings	51
Barbecue Chicken Drumsticks	52
Garlic Chicken Pizza	52
Chicken Tenders with Parmesan	53
Turkey Breast with Green Bean Casserole	53
Spicy Chicken Wings	54
Turkey Meatloaf	54
Chicken Fajitas & Street Corn	55
Crispy Prawns	55
Chicken with Pineapple Cauliflower Rice	56
Grilled Chicken Breasts	56
Chicken with Roasted Snap Peas	57
Chicken with Broccoli	58
Coconut Chicken Tenders	59
Chicken Fajitas	59
Spicy Chicken Sandwiches	60
Easy Chicken Thighs	60
Chicken with Potato Salad	61
Crusted Chicken	61
Ranch Turkey Tenders with Vegetable Salad	62
Maple-Mustard Glazed Turkey Tenderloin	62
Southern Fried Chicken	63
Crispy Butter Chicken	63
Breaded Chicken Breasts	64
Chicken Parmesan	64
Chicken Drumsticks with Sweet Rub	65
Fried Turkey Breast	65
Apricot Chicken	66
Dill Chicken Strips	66
Pecan-Crusted Chicken	67
Goat Cheese Stuffed Chicken Breast	67

68 ▶ Chapter 5 Seafood Recipes

Fish Fingers	68
Fish Fillet	68
Lemon Fish Fillets	69
Cod	69
Crab Croquettes	70
Halibut Steak	70
Broiled Tilapia Fillets	71
Onion Salmon Patties	71
Jumbo Prawns	71
Cheese Tilapia Fillets	72
Salmon Croquettes with Parsley	72
Bread-crumbed Fish	72
Cream Salmon	73
Prawns & Bacon Slices	73
Chunky Canned Fish	73
Asian Fish	74
Calamari Tubes	74
Crust Salmon	75
Parmesan Tilapia	75
Cajun Prawns	75
Salmon Fillets	76
Cajun Salmon	76
Breaded Salmon with Cheese	76

77 ▶ Chapter 6 Meat Recipes

T-bone Steak with Salsa	77
Honey Mustard Ham	77
Flank Steak with Peppers	78
Taco Pizza	78
Steak Fajitas	79
Pork Chops	79
Balsamic Marinated Rib Eye Steak	80
Spicy Grilled Steak	80
Beef Spinach Braciole	81
Rib Eye Cheesesteaks	82
Roast Beef with Potatoes	82
Cranberry Burgers	83
Beef & Broccoli	83
Beef Lettuce Wraps	84
Beef Cheese Empanadas	85
Meatballs in Tomato Sauce	86
Panko Boneless Pork Chops	86
Lemon Pork Tenderloin	87
Barbecued Back Ribs	87
Pork Teriyaki	88
Greek Lamb Burgers	88
Chicken Steak	89
Jerk-Flavoured Pork Loin	89

90 ▶ Chapter 7 Dessert Recipes

Brownies with Peanuts	90
Pistachio Pears	90
Apple & Berry Crumble	91
Jumbo Bar Cookie	91
Tasty Pear Pecan Crostata	92
Gingerbread Crusted Nuts	92
White Chocolate Blondies	93
Bread Pudding with Dried Fruits	93
Chocolate Lava Cake with Raspberry	94
Berries Pavlova	95
Mini Peanut Butter Cheesecake	95
Butter Gingerbread	96
Cream Puffs	96
Peppermint Bonbon Alaska	97
Bread Rolls	98
Pie Crust	99
Chocolate Doughnuts	99
Brown Sugar Cookies	100
Simple Cake	100
Chocolate Chip Cookie	100
Chilled Strawberry Pie	101
Chocolate Soufflés	101

102 ▶ Conclusion

103 ▶ Appendix Recipes Index

Introduction

The quick, effective, and oil-free cooking technology of air fryers has made it possible to eat tasty cuisine every day while maintaining a healthy lifestyle. I can't help but wonder what my life would have been like if I hadn't spent the past six years of my life cooking with air fryers. Even after a long day at work, I don't hate cooking at home because air fryers make regular cooking so easy and convenient; I try all my favourite dishes without worrying about adding extra calories. I've been able to maintain my weight while still enjoying all the crunchy appetizers, dinners, and desserts, thanks to air frying. I've had a great air-frying experience so far, and I want you to have that too! So here comes a perfect opportunity for you to try a wide variety of tasty and simple air fryer dishes from this cookbook to satisfy all of your dietary needs while maintaining good health.

Fundamental of Air Frying

What Is an Air Fryer?

An air fryer is a new-age cooking appliance which has gained popularity in this era as people are more concerned about health and nutrition. In today's world, people are more attentive and conscious to health and nutritional needs, as people are suffering from different types of chronic diseases. Foods cooked in more oil can increase weight. They have lower fat content as compared to common fried food, which makes them a good appliance for healthier cooking. With an air fryer, one can enjoy fried foods by cooking in less oil, which is not possible in an oven. In an air fryer, cooked food turns out to be more crispy and tender without loss of texture and flavor, which is not possible in deep-fried foods. They are more energy efficient, can cook ingredients quickly, and can save you both time and energy.

It is basically a hybrid between a fryer and a convection oven. It decreases the amount of oil absorbed into foods as compared to the deep fryer. It is generally beneficial for those who want to consume fewer calories, which ultimately reduce the risk of weight gain, obesity and some type of cancers.

When we compare air fryers to deep fryers, the air fryer is a healthier option because it has fewer calories and can result in less inflammation and may reduce the risk for chronic disease.

How Does an Air Fryer Work?

Convection heat is used in air fryers to cook food so that it is crispy and browned on the exterior but moist and soft on the inside. In comparison to deep frying or conventional oven roasting, cooking using an air fryer takes less time and creates less mess. Another benefit of air frying is that it consumes little oil.

In air fryers, food is cooked at temperatures approximately 400°F by hot air from above passing through perforated baskets, wire racks, and/or ceramic plates. This seals in the moisture and initially cooks the outside. Some models have pre-programmed settings that can instantly prepare common items if convenience is what you're after. Additionally, you might prefer digital controls for time and temperature regulation over analogue dials (think LEDs and touchscreens).

The names single- and dual-zone denote how many distinct cooking chambers are present in the apparatus. For use when you want more separation between products, such as when cooking chicken breasts or dehydrating fruits, several of these appliances also come with racks. Remember that you must provide enough space between items for good air circulation. If you stuff too much into the basket or onto the racks, the results won't be good. Food that is overcrowded will likely be soggy or cooked unevenly. You'll want to pay attention to the size and shape of the cooking area as well as the overall dimensions of the unit when choosing one that best fits your needs.

Drawer Pull-Out Air Fryer

Those types of air fryers require manual shaking of food every five to ten minutes to ensure even cooking of the food because some models don't have any time alert to alert you to shake your food. These models are not best for some foods like fish, meatballs and crumbed foods.

Stirrer

That type of air fryer has a paddle that gradually stirs the food during the cooking process. This self-stirring air fryer reduces the manual stir process and saves time. They are the best of foods like deep fried food and baked foods such as small meat and vegetables. Some of their models come with extra bowls without paddles which are more Suitable For Roasting Meat, Chicken And Baking Cake.

Rotating Basket Cooker

That type of air fryer is more versatile; they rotate the basket automatically. They include more accessories which can cook and allow you to cook the whole chicken.

What Can We Cook In an Air Fryer?

Usually, air fryers use dry heat for cooking foods like roasting and baking without or with less oil. First, air fryers were only popular for cooking pre-frozen foods like nuggets and chips but nowadays, as awareness increased and people know the importance for low oily food and the adverse effect of oil on health which increased the popularity of air fryers increased for more foods like vegetables, grilling fish, meat, chicken, cakes, desserts, granola and roasting nuts according to people choice and need. Before cooking food, people should know the cooking time of each meal to avoid burning food, as air fryers produce high temperatures in small places quickly.

Advantages of Using an Air Fryer

The first air fryer was created by Philips, who unveiled it in 2010 at a European consumer electronics expo. The category has expanded greatly since then. Over the past two years, in the USA alone more than 25 million air fryers have been sod, according to some estimates. The original brand name of Philips, Airfryer, is now used to refer to the entire category. Some other benefits of using an air fryer are:

Ease of cooking and cleaning
An air fryer is beneficial in most ways as compared to deep frying. Food can be cooked in 15 to 30 minutes, depending on the food, which ultimately can save you time. It can save time as some air fryers automatically stir features. They are easy to clean after cooking the food, unlike convection ovens, as all you have to wash is the basket and pan.

Quality of food
The quality of food can be maintained in the air fryer. Food can be easily cooked with no wastage of nutrients, and maintain the quality of food in less oil.

Preserve Nutrients
Some nutrients are lost during cooking, while air fryers contain air convection which helps in preserving certain nutrients. Some plants compounds like polyphenols which are present in green leafy vegetables and some other colored vegetables that have great protective health effects remain preserved in the air fryer

Food can be reheated
Air fryers are great for reheating food quickly without loss of flavor and texture. With different time adjustment features, food can be reheated quickly. They can keep the food crispy, not soggy, like pizza and battered foods.

Help in Weight management
Deep-fried food can be dangerous to health. Food that is deeply cooked in oil has negative health outcomes as we all know that deep-fried food has a lot of calories which has a direct link to obesity. Oil-containing foods lose their nutritional values and sometimes flavour too. Therefore switching from deep-fried food to air-fried foods and reducing the intake of unhealthy oil can help in weight loss. Air fryer requires less oil as compared to deep fryers need; people can still enjoy a healthy meal that has the same flavors and texture.

Help in disease management
People with chronic diseases such as heart disease, diabetes, obese cant consume foods that are cooked in oil, as oily foods can increase cholesterol levels, which ultimately prone them to more diseases. So people with chronic diseases can take benefits from air fryers in moderation and keeping their portion size small. By cooking or grilling food in moderate amounts in the air fryer, those people can enjoy their meals without any negative health outcomes. Lower oil intake can be a lot of benefits as low oil intake is linked with a lot of heart disease. It can help with diabetes, weight management in adults and some stomach problems.

Safe to Use
Foods that are deep fried contain a lot of scalding oil, which has a lot of health risks, while an air fryer has a large heating container which has no spilling or touching of hot oil

No Risk Of Toxic Acrylamide Formation
As we know that deep fried food contains a compound called dietary acrylamide, which is

classified as human carcinogenic, meaning, it can develop cancer. This compound is present in foods that are rich in carbohydrates. This compound is formed during high cooking of fried foods like deep frying of food. Substance acrylamide is toxic to health as it can develop some types of cancers such as endometrial, ovarian, pancreatic, breast and oesophagal cancer. According to research, acrylamide development has a link with these types of cancer. Therefore by switching to air fryers, people can reduce the risk of developing acrylamide in food.

Air-fried foods can reduce disease risk

As we know that cooking food in oil and its consumption on a regular basis are linked with many diseases. Replacing deep frying with other cooking methods can reduce disease risk without any complications, and enjoy meals.

Is an Air fryer Worth It?

Donuts, cookies, potato or vegetable chips, fresh or frozen french fries and sweet potato fries, pizza, and burgers can all be made at home by indulgent home cooks. And if you prefer convenience to anything else, utilizing an air fryer instead of a standard oven will help you cook your favourite frozen foods faster and with crispier results. Air fryer is best for:

- Hostel students
- People living in small houses having small kitchens
- People who have a small kitchen or have no oven
- People on a diet or having high BMI
- People who have high blood lipid profile, especially cholesterol, triglyceride, low-density lipoprotein and high-density lipoprotein.
- Those who enjoy crispy food such as vegetable chips

What to Look, When Buying an Air Fryer?

When selecting an air fryer, it's important to think about how you'll use it, what foods you'll cook in it, how many people you'll feed, how much counter space you have, and how sensitive you are to noise and heat. Aesthetics are an additional consideration because it will probably reside on your countertop. Before buying an air fryer, one should keep in mind the following,

Size and Capacity

Air fryers have different sizes, so before buying an air fryer, you can determine what you cook and how much you cook. Therefore it's also important before buying an air fryer; you should already know where to put it in the kitchen. Machines like air fryers need some counter space, so clearing a place for them would be best. So always keep in mind that air fryers run on electricity, and they should be placed near an outlet for them to work.

The bigger the size of the air fryer, the bigger the capacity it will have. The capacity of an air fryer is based on how many litres of food it can accommodate. Air fryers come in a range of different sizes, including small fryers (with a capacity of 1-2 litres), medium-sized fryers (with 1.8-2.5 litres), to larges-sized fryers (around 5 litres and above), and some contain a capacity of up to 23 liters (Hanabishi air fryer). In terms of quartz, the cooking capacity of the air fryers starts from 4 quarts to up to 8-10 quarts. If you have a small family or a small kitchen, then you will need a small air fryer.

Wattage

Most kitchen wattage range between 800 to 1500 watts; therefore, before buying an air fryer, you must know the knowing the wattage of your air fryer; it would help you with both safety and the cooking itself. Some of the air fryers usually have higher wattage of air fryers which can come at 1800 watts or more. A larger air fryer can hotter quickly, which can save time by cooking meals faster. This is enough for baking cake, whole chicken and restaurant purposes.

Energy Consumption

They are efficient, so they can cook within 15 minutes for most foods and 30 minutes of cooking time for tougher meats, and that uses only half a unit of electricity compared to electric ovens and other electric cooking appliances.

Temperature Settings

Different air fryers have different temperature

settings; it also depends on the food that is cooked in the air fryer. Some food requires high temperatures than others foods. White meat, like chicken, requires less temperature as compared to red meat, like meatballs require a temperature of around 204°C (400°F); however, foods like potato chips and pasta require less temperature.

Safety

an air fryer is an electrical machine it can get hot during cooking food or in a small kitchen or hot environment, which can be dangerous for health. So air fryers should be kept in an area where you have a good air exhaust system, so they can get hotter quickly. Air fryers should be only used by adults.

Budget

air fryers are available at different prices, ranging from $100 to $122. Their prices are equal to gas stoves, but air fryers are more convenient than gas stoves and environmentally friendly, as you would not need any gas to cook the food oil.

Additional Features

Some air fryers come with features of dehydrators; if you like dehydrated foods, then these are good options for you. Some air fryers have features like the toaster and even rotisserie functions. It can be perfect if you like to toast bread or you want to cook rotisserie chicken.

Straight from the Store

You should take off all of the stickers and the air fryer's packing before using it for the first time. After that, place it on a solid, heat-resistant surface. Make sure the air fryer is set up far from other surfaces and items. This will stop heat coming from the air fryer from doing any harm. You should remove the basket from the air fryer using the handle in order to get rid of all the plastic packaging. Use the basket release button to separate the inner and outer baskets. Use a non-abrasive sponge or a dishwasher to thoroughly clean both baskets. With a slightly moist towel, clean the basket's interior and outside. The basket can be dried with a dry towel. After that, return the basket to the air fryer.

Test run of the air fryer

Before using the air fryer for cooking, you should test it at least once. This will help you in becoming familiar with the various features of your air fryer and ensure that it is operating properly. The air fryer can be examined as follows:

1. Connect the air fryer's power plug. The entire air fryer basket should be used. Next, give the air fryer some time to warm up. You will see a preheat button on your air fryer if it has multiple functions. Small, pricey air fryers typically use analogue control systems. These will need to be manually warmed up in order to manually preheat and heat for 5 minutes at 400°F.

2. When the preheating process is finished, the air fryer will beep. After that, remove the air fryer's basket and give it five minutes to cool. After that, replace the empty basket inside the air fryer. Decide on the time and temperature you want. Now check to see if the air fryer is operating properly.

3. The air fryer will automatically switch off and keep making the "beep" sound when the cooking time is up. Then, using the handle, remove the air fryer basket, allowing it to cool for 10 to 30 minutes. If everything goes as planned, your air fryer will be ready for use.

Tips for the Air Fryer Basket

Only remove the air fryer's basket when adding and removing food. Avoid repeatedly removing the basket. The handle's button guard stops the user from unintentionally hitting the release button. To release the basket, slide the button guard forward.

When taking out the basket, never hit the basket release button. This is because the basket may fall and create mishaps if the release button is pressed while the basket is being carried. When you're ready, merely press the basket release button. Make sure the surface you plan to set it on is secure and heat-resistant. The air fryer's handle is affixed to the inside basket rather than the outside basket. As a result, your outer basket will drop when you press the release button on the basket.

Anything placed on top of the air fryer will block the airflow. So, the meal may not cook perfectly. Keep in mind that an air fryer differs from a deep fryer. This implies that no additional oil is needed when using an air fryer. Actually, it's not a good idea to cook extremely fatty meals in an air fryer.

It is necessary to heat up the air fryer before using it for cooking. This is done so that once the air fryer is preheated, the food will cook more quickly and have a crispy exterior. A multi-purpose device can be instantly preheated by pressing the preheat button. However, manual preheating is required for little, low-cost air fryers. The air fryer needs to be manually preheated for five minutes at 400°f.

After the air fryer has finished preheating, remove the air fryer basket and add the food. However, keep in mind that the basket shouldn't include too much food. Because if the basket is overfilled, the food may not be cooked properly.

After adding food to the air fryer basket, place it inside the appliance. Next, decide when and at what temperature meals should be served. While cooking, you can also change the temperature and time.

Press the "start" button to begin air frying. But after you start cooking, you have to keep an eye on it to make sure it doesn't get too done or burnt. You can combine the ingredients midway through cooking or flip the meal over to ensure that it is thoroughly cooked. When the cooking time is up, the air fryer will beep.

Next, take out the air fryer basket. But mind the heat of the steam. After separating the inner and outer baskets, serve the food. Separate the inner from the outer basket while keeping the basket on a flat surface. The basket must completely cool before cleaning.

Cleaning and Caring for Your Air Fryer

There are several different types of air fryers available. It is also best to always examine the owner's manual for detailed instructions about your air fryer. However, generally speaking, the simplest approach to clean an air fryer is to give it a quick cleaning at least once every other usage. If you prepare something extremely messy, like something with sauce or marinade, clean it the same day; otherwise, you may wind up with a stuck-on mess. It gets tougher to clean off something sticky the longer it sits in the air fryer. Cleaning your air fryer periodically will not only make the task simpler, but it will also stop the accumulation of food particles that could result in odors, malfunctions, or even, worst case scenario, a fire. The simplest method for lightly cleaning your air fryer is as follows:

● Let your fryer cool down after using it, then unplug it.
● The basket, pan, or tray should be removed and washed in the sink with warm water and dish soap. Overnight drying is recommended.
● With a damp sponge, soapy cloth, or paper towel, clean the interior of the fryer, paying special attention to the heating element. Reclean the area with a moist towel, then dry it off.
● Use a gentle towel to clean the fryer's outside.
● Place the removable fryer parts inside the fryer once they are dry.
● Avoid using abrasive cleaners and scrubbers on your air fryer since they could scratch the nonstick components and body.

Air Fryer Be Deep Cleaning
With a few more steps, the procedure is essentially the same as the light cleaning you perform after cooking. Air fryers are essentially little convection ovens with a nonstick drawer, so if you have caked-on food, you may treat it much like you would a nonstick pan. Adding a cup of water to your air fryer basket, turning it on high for a few minutes, and then leaving it alone will help to remove cooked-on grease and debris. When you open the drawer, you'll

see that a lot of dirt and grime washed out without any effort or soap.

The full-air fryer should never be submerged in water. If your air fryer's removable parts are still grimy after soaking in hot, soapy water for about 30 minutes, gently scrub them with a toothbrush with a soft bristle. A toothpick can also be used to (gently) reach areas that are difficult to clean, such as the grate's perforations. Do not put the removable parts of your air fryer in the dishwasher, even if the manual suggests it.

Getting Rid of Sticky Residue

Making a thick paste with a little bit of water and around a half cup of baking soda will help you remove the stickiest, toughest gunk from the inside of your fryer. Apply the paste over the sticky areas, then wait a few minutes before removing it with a soft-bristled toothbrush. Dry off the interior of the fryer after wiping it off with a moist cloth.

Tips for Air Frying

1. Although some foods don't necessarily require it, I prefer to add oils to some foods to make them crispy. You really don't need oil if your diet already contains some fat (dark flesh chicken, ground beef, fatty cuts of meat, etc.).

2. Even if your cuisine doesn't require oil, spend a moment greasing the air fryer's container. I grease mine by rubbing or brushing some oil onto the underneath of the grates.

3. Never use aerosol spray cans in an air fryer. Numerous air fryer containers have been known to chip when used with aerosol spray cans, including those from pam and comparable companies. The harmful chemicals in aerosol cans don't match the materials used to cover the majority of the containers.

4. Avoid packing the refrigerator to the brim if you want your fried food to come out fresh. If you put too much food in the air fryer basket, it won't cook evenly and brown as it should. To prevent this, prepare your food in batches or purchase a larger air fryer.

5. While frying small foods such as chicken wings and French fries, shake the basket regularly to guarantee even cooking. Occasionally, use a pair of silicone kitchen tongs to flip over larger items and shake the basket to ensure even cooking. The air fryer will pause briefly when you shake the basket, but it will resume cooking the food at the same temperature when you return the basket.

6. Spray halfway through cooking: I have found that for the majority of dishes, spraying oil halfway through cooking works well. I usually wait to spray until the middle of cooking unless it's an ingredient that doesn't require it, like fatty meats. Food items with coatings should be sprayed with oil.

7. Stop white smoke with water or bread in the base. When using your air fryer for cooking oily food, don't be alarmed if you notice some white smoke coming from the appliance. Simply pour some water (2 tablespoons) into the bottom of the container to fix the issue. The smoke will go out while the food continues to cook. When cooking foods that can spread a lot of fat, like bacon, some people place a slice of bread in the bottom of the pan to absorb the grease.

8. Watch out for the small light items in the air fryer: the top of the majority of air fryer units houses a strong fan. Due to this, some items of lighter weight may be dangerously swept up in the fan.

9. Change the temperature: In order to get the air fryer to operate, you usually want to increase the heat up to the highest setting. However, you should exercise caution because some foods will dry out quickly at this temperature. A suitable method calls for varying the temperature and duration from what you would typically do in the oven. I like to reduce the temperature by 30 degrees and the time by roughly 20%. To start, reduce the temperature in the air fryer to 320°F and cook it for roughly 16 minutes; if you made brownies at 350°F in the oven for 20 minutes. At times, an air fryer combo is preferable.

10. Buy a good quality thermometer. When it comes to cooking poultry, fish, and pork in your air fryer, having a high-quality, quick-read thermometer is crucial.

1. How many meals may be prepared in a batch?

This is based on the air fryer's dimensions and capacity. However, it is not advised to completely fill the air fryer basket because doing so will impede the flow of hot air inside. Food that has been cooked unevenly as a result of this.

Per batch, the basket should not be filled more than halfway. Because of this, a typical air fryer can hold two to three meals. You should also consult the owner's handbook and the recipe book that came with your particular model. These typically list the suggested batch sizes for each kind of food you can bake or cook.

2. Do pan-fried and deep-fried foods taste different from those that are air-fried?

The texture and flavour of food that has been air-fried should be identical to food that has been traditionally fried, ideally. The interior might be soft or sensitive, while the exterior is golden and crispy. Food that has been air-fried should, at most, be lighter because less oil has been used to prepare it. The differences, however, would be highlighted depending on the cooking technique, such as the usage of oil sprayers instead of a brush and the type of breading used to coat the food.

3. What stores sell air fryers?

Since air fryers have become more and more popular recently, you can now buy one from any big appliance retailer. There are many different brands and types to pick from, so you should carefully study reviews from people who already own the aforementioned air fryer. For each model you are considering, make a note of the unique features, available accessories, and servicing warranty.

4. Do I need any extras to use the air fryer for baking or cooking?

Although it is not necessary, using particular accessories might enhance the outcome or reduce the amount of time needed to cook. Check to see if these accessories are compatible with a specific air fryer model before even considering purchasing them. Typically, the manufacturer sells add-ons that are restricted to users with the brands they sell. A grill mat, which may keep the basket clear of burned food particles, and a baking dish, which is mostly used to prepare saucy dishes, are typical examples of air fryer accessories.

5. Do I have to add oil to the food for air frying?

When you are using an air fryer, you only need up to 1 tablespoon of oil for every kilogramme of fresh food. Although oil gives food flavour, it is not necessary for cooking pre-cooked frozen items. You can use an oil mister to add a light layer of oil over the food. This light layer is only there to prevent the food from completely drying out during cooking.

6. Can I reheat the cooked food in an air fryer?

Reheating food in air fryers is excellent if you want to preserve its crispiness and avoid making it mushy, such as with pizza and items that have been battered. These days most new air fryers come with a "reheat" preset which is perfect for doing so. If there is no such preset, then simply set the temperature to 325°F and reheat the food for 3-5 minutes.

7. In an air fryer, how many chips can you make?

Depending on the cooking capacity of an air fryer, you can cook between 1 lb. and 2 lbs. of chips, which is plenty for 2-4 people.

8. Can I use foil and baking paper in an air fryer?

Before using foil or baking paper in your air fryer, always verify the manufacturer's instructions. Although it is conceivable, you should exercise caution and think about how it can affect the final product. Because covering the bottom of the basket with baking paper or foil could disrupt and reduce airflow, affecting cooking performance, several manufacturers advise against doing so.

4-Week Meal Plan

Week 1

Day 1:
Breakfast: Chocolate Chip Muffins
Lunch: Marinated Tofu Cubes
Snack: Courgette Sticks
Dinner: Lemon-Pepper Chicken Thighs
Dessert: Brownies with Peanuts

Day 2:
Breakfast: Super-Filling Calzones
Lunch: Crispy Tofu & Sweet Potato
Snack: Simple Courgette
Dinner: Fish Fingers
Dessert: Apple & Berry Crumble

Day 3:
Breakfast: Ham Eggs
Lunch: Stuffed Potatoes with Dressing
Snack: Tamari Aubergine
Dinner: Barbecue Chicken Drumsticks
Dessert: Jumbo Bar Cookie

Day 4:
Breakfast: Chopped Blueberry Muffins
Lunch: Homemade Giant Nachos
Snack: Glazed Carrots
Dinner: T-bone Steak with Salsa
Dessert: Tasty Pear Pecan Crostata

Day 5:
Breakfast: Vanilla Cinnamon Rolls
Lunch: Potato-Stuffed Peppers
Snack: Fried Green Tomatoes
Dinner: Jumbo Prawns
Dessert: Gingerbread Crusted Nuts

Day 6:
Breakfast: Cheese Pepper Eggs
Lunch: Avocado Tacos
Snack: Low-Fat Buffalo Cauliflower
Dinner: Asian Fish
Dessert: White Chocolate Blondies

Day 7:
Breakfast: Tomato Egg White Cups
Lunch: Lemon Aubergine Dip
Snack: Onion Rings
Dinner: Flank Steak with Peppers
Dessert: Pistachio Pears

Week 2

Day 1:
Breakfast: Simple Muffins
Lunch: Mini Mushroom-Onion Pizzas
Snack: Roasted Shishito Peppers
Dinner: Chicken Fajitas & Street Corn
Dessert: Bread Pudding with Dried Fruits

Day 2:
Breakfast: Cheddar Spinach Omelet
Lunch: Breaded White Mushrooms
Snack: Kale Chips
Dinner: Crispy Prawns
Dessert: Chocolate Lava Cake with Raspberry

Day 3:
Breakfast: Cheese Soufflés
Lunch: Broccoli Salad
Snack: Garlic Tortilla Chips
Dinner: Beef Spinach Braciole
Dessert: Berries Pavlova

Day 4:
Breakfast: Fluffy Bacon Quiche
Lunch: Vegan Sandwiches
Snack: Sweet Potato Chips
Dinner: Chicken with Roasted Snap Peas
Dessert: Butter Gingerbread

Day 5:
Breakfast: Sausage Meatballs
Lunch: Cheese Bean Taquitos
Snack: Simple French Fries
Dinner: Onion Salmon Patties
Dessert: Cream Puffs

Day 6:
Breakfast: Turkey Burgers
Lunch: Quinoa Patties
Snack: French Fries with Shallots
Dinner: Taco Pizza
Dessert: Peppermint Bonbon Alaska

Day 7:
Breakfast: Tasty Sausage-Crusted Egg Cups
Lunch: Cheese Vegetarian Lasagna
Snack: Berbere-Spiced Potato Fries
Dinner: Greek Lamb Burgers
Dessert: Bread Rolls

Week 3

Day 1:
Breakfast: Cute Bagels
Lunch: Barbecue Pulled Jackfruit
Snack: Glazed Brussels Sprouts
Dinner: Beef Lettuce Wraps
Dessert: Pie Crust

Day 2:
Breakfast: Jalapeño & Bacon Pizza
Lunch: Chili Dogs
Snack: "Samosas" with Coriander Chutney
Dinner: Lemon Fish Fillets
Dessert: Mini Peanut Butter Cheesecake

Day 3:
Breakfast: Savory Egg Pizza
Lunch: Avocado Rice Bowls
Snack: Indian Okra
Dinner: Chicken with Broccoli
Dessert: Chocolate Doughnuts

Day 4:
Breakfast: Vanilla Pancakes
Lunch: Cauliflower Steak
Snack: Pakoras
Dinner: Spicy Chicken Wings
Dessert: Chocolate Soufflés

Day 5:
Breakfast: Cinnamon Pecan Granola
Lunch: Cheese Courgette Boats
Snack: Spring Rolls
Dinner: Lemon Fish Fillet
Dessert: Chilled Strawberry Pie

Day 6:
Breakfast: Yummy Jalapeño Egg Cups
Lunch: Mini Portobello Pizzas
Snack: Garlic Russet Potatoes
Dinner: Pork Chops
Dessert: Brown Sugar Cookies

Day 7:
Breakfast: Quinoa Quiche
Lunch: Vegetable Quesadilla
Snack: Easy-to-Cook Asparagus
Dinner: Chicken with Potato Salad
Dessert: Chocolate Chip Cookie

Week 4

Day 1:
Breakfast: French Whole-Grain Toast
Lunch: Spinach & Artichoke Casserole
Snack: Fast-Cooked Courgette Rolls
Dinner: Cajun Prawns
Dessert: Simple Cake

Day 2:
Breakfast: Fruit Muffins
Lunch: Cheese Zoodle
Snack: Parmesan Courgette Chips
Dinner: Meatballs in Tomato Sauce
Dessert: Brownies with Peanuts

Day 3:
Breakfast: Oat Bowls
Lunch: Stuffed Aubergine
Snack: Seasoned Sweet Potato Wedges
Dinner: Breaded Salmon with Cheese
Dessert: Apple & Berry Crumble

Day 4:
Breakfast: Homemade Hash Browns
Lunch: Broccoli Salad
Snack: Savoury Potato Wedges
Dinner: Crispy Butter Chicken
Dessert: Jumbo Bar Cookie

Day 5:
Breakfast: Apple-Cinnamon Cookies
Lunch: Roasted Lemon Cauliflower
Snack: Onion Rings
Dinner: Chunky Canned Fish
Dessert: Tasty Pear Pecan Crostata

Day 6:
Breakfast: Tofu Scramble Brunch
Lunch: Cauliflower Pizza Crust
Snack: Courgette Sticks
Dinner: Dill Chicken Strips
Dessert: Gingerbread Crusted Nuts

Day 7:
Breakfast: Special Patties
Lunch: Veggie Bowl
Snack: Glazed Carrots
Dinner: Barbecued Back Ribs
Dessert: White Chocolate Blondies

Chapter 1 Breakfast Recipes

Chocolate Chip Muffins

Prep time: 5 minutes | Cook time: 15 minutes | Serves: 6

150g blanched finely ground almond flour
50g granular brown erythritol
4 tablespoons salted butter, melted

2 large eggs, whisked
1 tablespoon baking powder
85g chocolate chips

1. Combine all of the ingredients in a large mixing bowl. 2. Grease six silicone muffin cups with cooking spray, and then divide the batter among them. 3. Arrange the cups into the air fryer basket, and then cook the food at 160°C on Bake mode for 15 minutes until they are golden brown. 4. Let muffins cool in cups 15 minutes to avoid crumbling. Serve warm.

Per Serving: Calories 379; Fat 32.27g; Sodium 287mg; Carbs 12.97g; Fibre 4.7g; Sugar 4.01g; Protein 14.11g

Super-Filling Calzones

Prep time: 15 minutes | Cook time: 12 minutes | Serves: 4

2 large eggs
100g blanched finely ground almond flour
280g shredded mozzarella cheese

50g cream cheese, softened and broken into small pieces
4 slices cooked bacon, crumbled

1. Beat eggs in a small bowl, then pour into a medium nonstick frying pan over medium heat and scramble. Set aside. 2. Mix flour and mozzarella in a large microwave-safe bowl, and then add the cream cheese to it. 3. Microwave the mozzarella mixture for 45 seconds on high to melt cheese, then stir with a fork until a soft dough ball forms. 4. Separate dough into two sections and press each out into an 20 cm round; on half of each dough round, place half of the scrambled eggs and crumbled bacon. Fold the other side of the dough over and press to seal the edges. 5. Line the air fryer basket with parchment paper, and then place the calzones on it. 6. Air-fry the calzones at 175°C for 12 minutes until the crusts are golden and firm, turning them over halfway through cooking. 7. Let calzones cool on a cooking rack 5 minutes before serving.

Per Serving: Calories 425; Fat 29.51g; Sodium 718mg; Carbs 9.62g; Fibre 4.6g; Sugar 3.1g; Protein 33.72g

Vanilla Cinnamon Rolls

Prep time: 10 minutes | Cook time: 20 minutes | Serves: 12

310g shredded mozzarella cheese	½ teaspoon vanilla extract
50g cream cheese, softened	80g erythritol
100g blanched finely ground almond flour	1 tablespoon ground cinnamon

1. Whisk the mozzarella cheese, cream cheese, and flour in a large microwave-safe bowl. 2. Microwave the mixture on high 90 seconds until cheese is melted. 3. Add vanilla extract and erythritol, and mix them for 2 minutes until a dough forms. 4. Once the dough is cool enough to work with your hands, spread it out into a suitable rectangle on ungreased parchment paper. Evenly sprinkle dough with cinnamon. 5. Starting at the long side of the dough, roll lengthwise to form a log. Slice the log into twelve even pieces. 6. Divide rolls between two ungreased baking dishes. 7. Air-fry the pieces at 190°C for 10 minutes until they are golden around the edges and mostly firm. You can cook them in batches. 8. Allow rolls to cool in dishes 10 minutes before serving.

Per Serving: Calories 159; Fat 9.76g; Sodium 204mg; Carbs 8.54g; Fibre 2g; Sugar 5.86g; Protein 10.57g

Cute Bagels

Prep time: 5 minutes | Cook time: 10 minutes | Serves: 6

200g blanched finely ground almond flour	1½ teaspoons baking powder
280g shredded mozzarella cheese	1 teaspoon apple cider vinegar
3 tablespoons salted butter, divided	2 large eggs, divided

1. Combine the flour, mozzarella, and 1 tablespoon of butter in a large microwave-safe bowl. 2. Microwave the butter mixture on high 90 seconds, and then form into a soft ball of dough. 3. Add baking powder, vinegar, and 1 egg to dough, stirring until fully combined. 4. Once dough is cool enough to work with your hands, divide evenly into six balls. 5. Poke a hole in each ball of dough with your finger and gently stretch each ball out to be 5 cm in diameter. 6. Melt remaining butter in microwave on high 30 seconds, and then let cool 1 minute. Whisk with remaining egg, and then brush mixture over each bagel. 7. Line air fryer basket with parchment paper, and place bagels onto it, working in batches if needed. 8. Air-fry the bagels at 175°C for 10 minutes, flipping them halfway through cooking. 9. Allow the bagels cool for 15 minutes after cooking. 10. The leftovers can be refrigerated in the sealed bag for up to 4 days.

Per Serving: Calories 392; Fat 30.71g; Sodium 324mg; Carbs 11.14g; Fibre 5.5g; Sugar 2.83g; Protein 23.22g

Simple Muffins

Prep time: 5 minutes | Cook time: 15 minutes | Serves: 6

100g blanched finely ground almond flour

4 granular erythritol

2 tablespoons salted butter, melted

1 large egg, whisked

2 teaspoons baking powder

1 teaspoon ground allspice

1. Mix up all ingredients in a large bowl. 2. Grease six silicone muffin cups with cooking spray, and then divide the batter among them. 3. Arrange the cups into the air fryer basket, and then cook the food at 160°C on Bake mode for 15 minutes until they are golden brown. 4. Let muffins cool in cups 15 minutes to avoid crumbling. Serve warm.

Per Serving: Calories 209; Fat 18.06g; Sodium 200mg; Carbs 6.02g; Fibre 2.5g; Sugar 1.16g; Protein 9.02g

Ham Eggs

Prep time: 5 minutes | Cook time: 15 minutes | Serves: 2

3 large eggs

1 tablespoon salted butter, melted

35g seeded and chopped green pepper

2 tablespoons peeled and chopped yellow onion

70g chopped cooked ham

¼ teaspoon salt

¼ teaspoon ground black pepper

1. Crack eggs into an ungreased nonstick baking dish. Mix in butter, pepper, onion, ham, salt, and black pepper. 2. Arrange the dish into air fryer basket. 3. Air-fry the mixture at 160°C for 15 minutes until the eggs are fully cooked and firm in the middle. 4. Slice in half and serve warm on two medium plates.

Per Serving: Calories 153; Fat 11.58g; Sodium 698mg; Carbs 3.2g; Fibre 0.3g; Sugar 1.15g; Protein 9.21g

Chopped Blueberry Muffins

Prep time: 5 minutes | Cook time: 15 minutes | Serves: 6

150g blanched finely ground almond flour

80g granular erythritol

4 tablespoons salted butter, melted

2 large eggs, whisked

2 teaspoons baking powder

50g fresh blueberries, chopped

1. Combine all ingredients in a large bowl. 2. Grease six silicone muffin cups with cooking spray, and then divide the batter among them. 3. Arrange the cups into the air fryer basket, and then cook the food at 160°C on Bake mode for 15 minutes until they are golden brown. 4. Let muffins cool in cups 15 minutes to avoid crumbling. Serve warm.

Per Serving: Calories 356; Fat 29.77g; Sodium 397mg; Carbs 11.65g; Fibre 3.9g; Sugar 4.63g; Protein 15.5g

Cheese Pepper Eggs

Prep time: 10 minutes | Cook time: 15 minutes | Serves: 4

4 medium green peppers, tops removed, seeded
1 tablespoon coconut oil
75g chopped cooked ham
40g peeled and chopped white onion

4 large eggs
½ teaspoon salt
100g shredded mild Cheddar cheese

1. Place peppers upright into ungreased air fryer basket. 2. Spray each pepper with coconut oil. 3. Divide ham and onion among peppers. 4. Beat the eggs with salt in a medium bowl, and then evenly pour the mixture into each pepper. 5. Top each pepper with 25g of Cheddar cheese. 6. Air-fry the food at 160°C for 15 minutes until the peppers are tender and the eggs are firm. 7. Serve warm.

Per Serving: Calories 203; Fat 12.2g; Sodium 833mg; Carbs 10.51g; Fibre 1.2g; Sugar 5.01g; Protein 13.57g

Tomato Egg White Cups

Prep time: 10 minutes | Cook time: 15 minutes | Serves: 4

485g 100% liquid egg whites
3 tablespoons salted butter, melted
¼ teaspoon salt

¼ teaspoon onion powder
½ medium Roma tomato, cored and diced
15g chopped fresh spinach leaves

1. Whisk egg whites with butter, salt, and onion powder in a large bowl. Stir in tomato and spinach. 2. Grease four ramekins with cooking spray, and then pour the mixture evenly into them. 3. Arrange the ramekins into the air fryer basket. 4. Air-fry the food at 150°C for 15 minutes until the eggs are firm in the centre. 5. Serve warm.

Per Serving: Calories 117; Fat 5.86g; Sodium 446mg; Carbs 3.94g; Fibre 0.8g; Sugar 2.95g; Protein 12.92g

Cheddar Spinach Omelet

Prep time: 5 minutes | Cook time: 12 minutes | Serves: 2

4 large eggs
45g chopped fresh spinach leaves
2 tablespoons peeled and chopped yellow onion

2 tablespoons salted butter, melted
50g shredded mild Cheddar cheese
¼ teaspoon salt

1.Whisk the eggs in the ungreased baking dish directly, and then stir in the spinach, onion, butter, Cheddar, and salt. 2. Air-fry the mixture at 160°C for 12 minutes until the top is browned and the middle is firm. 3. Slice the omelet in half and serve warm.

Per Serving: Calories 298; Fat 20.33g; Sodium 894mg; Carbs 9.62g; Fibre 3.6g; Sugar 3.56g; Protein 20.8g

Cheese Soufflés

Prep time: 15 minutes | Cook time: 12 minutes | Serves: 4

3 large eggs, whites and yolks separated
¼ teaspoon cream of tartar

50g shredded sharp Cheddar cheese
75 gcream cheese, softened

1. Beat egg whites with cream of tartar in a bowl for 2 minutes until soft peaks form. 2. Beat egg yolks, Cheddar, and cream cheese together in another bowl for 1 minute until frothy; add egg yolk mixture to whites, gently folding until combined. 3. Grease four ramekins with cooking spray, and divide the mixture among them. 4. Arrange the ramekins into the air fryer basket, and then air-fry the food at 175°C for 12 minutes. When done, the top should be browned and the centre should be firm. 5. Serve and enjoy.

Per Serving: Calories 162; Fat 14.26g; Sodium 190mg; Carbs 1.63g; Fibre 0g; Sugar 0.85g; Protein 6.97g

Fluffy Bacon Quiche

Prep time: 5 minutes | Cook time: 12 minutes | Serves: 2

3 large eggs
2 tablespoons heavy whipping cream
¼ teaspoon salt

4 slices cooked bacon, crumbled
50g shredded mild Cheddar cheese

1. Whisk the eggs, cream, and salt in a bowl until combined, and then mix in the bacon and Cheddar. 2. Apportion the mixture between two ungreased ramekins, and then place them in the air fryer basket. 3. Air-fry the food at 160°C for 12 minutes until they are fluffy and set in the middle. 4. Let the dish cool for 5 minutes after cooking, and then enjoy.

Per Serving: Calories 291; Fat 22.91g; Sodium 1008mg; Carbs 4.76g; Fibre 0g; Sugar 2.56g; Protein 15.96g

Vanilla Pancakes

Prep time: 5 minutes | Cook time: 30 minutes | Serves: 2

100g blanched finely ground almond flour
2 tablespoons granular erythritol
1 tablespoon salted butter, melted

1 large egg
80ml unsweetened almond milk
½ teaspoon vanilla extract

1. Combine all ingredients in a large bowl, and then pour half the batter into an ungreased baking dish. 2. Air-fry the batter at 160°C for 15 minutes until golden brown on top and firm, and a toothpick inserted in the centre will come out clean when done. Do the same with the remaining batter. 3. Slice in half in dish and serve warm.

Per Serving: Calories 554; Fat 47.5g; Sodium 317mg; Carbs 18.33g; Fibre 8g; Sugar 7g; Protein 21.09g

Sausage Meatballs

Prep time: 10 minutes | Cook time: 15 minutes | Serves: 6

455g pork breakfast sausage meat
½ teaspoon salt
¼ teaspoon ground black pepper

50g shredded sharp Cheddar cheese
25g cream cheese, softened
1 large egg, whisked

1. Combine all ingredients in a large bowl. Form mixture into eighteen 2.5cm meatballs. 2. Place meatballs into the ungreased air fryer basket. 3. Air-fry the meatballs at 205°C for 15 minutes until they have an internal temperature of at least 60°C, shaking basket three times during cooking. 4. Serve warm.
Per Serving: Calories 305; Fat 27.03g; Sodium 965mg; Carbs 2.48g; Fibre 0g; Sugar 0.3g; Protein 12.19g

Turkey Burgers

Prep time: 5 minutes | Cook time: 15 minutes | Serves: 4

455g turkey breakfast sausage meat
½ teaspoon salt
¼ teaspoon ground black pepper

35g seeded and chopped green pepper
2 tablespoons mayonnaise
1 medium avocado, peeled, pitted, and sliced

1. Mix the sausage with salt, black pepper, pepper, and mayonnaise in a large bowl. Form four patties from the mixture. 2. Arrange the patties into ungreased air fryer basket, and then air-fry them at 190°C for 15 minutes until they are dark brown and have an internal temperature of at least 75°C, turning them halfway through cooking. 3. Serve burgers topped with avocado slices.
Per Serving: Calories 373; Fat 30.28g; Sodium 1077mg; Carbs 6.82g; Fibre 3.5g; Sugar 0.68g; Protein 19.05g

Tasty Sausage–Crusted Egg Cups

Prep time: 10 minutes | Cook time: 15 minutes | Serves: 6

150g pork breakfast sausage meat
6 large eggs
½ teaspoon salt

¼ teaspoon ground black pepper
½ teaspoon crushed red pepper flakes

1. Grease six 10 cm ramekins with cooking oil and divide the sausage among them. 2. Press sausage down to cover bottom and about 1 cm up the sides of ramekins. 3. Crack one egg into each ramekin and sprinkle evenly with salt, black pepper, and red pepper flakes. 4. Place the ramekins into air fryer basket, and then air-fry the food at 175°C for 15 minutes until the eggs are firm. 5. Serve warm.
Per Serving: Calories 317; Fat 25.33g; Sodium 1392mg; Carbs 1.74g; Fibre 0.1g; Sugar 0.38g; Protein 19.22g

Jalapeño & Bacon Pizza

Prep time: 5 minutes | Cook time: 10 minutes | Serves: 2

120g shredded mozzarella cheese
25g cream cheese, broken into small pieces
4 slices cooked bacon, chopped

20g chopped pickled jalapeños
1 large egg, whisked
¼ teaspoon salt

1. Place mozzarella in a single layer on the bottom of an ungreased baking dish. 2. Scatter cream cheese pieces, bacon, and jalapeños over mozzarella, and then pour egg evenly around baking dish, and sprinkle them with salt. 3. Air-fry the food at 165°C for 10 minutes until the cheese is brown and the egg is set. 4. Let the dish cool on a large plate for 5 minutes before serving.
Per Serving: Calories 376; Fat 24.81g; Sodium 1470mg; Carbs 10.048g; Fibre 1.1g; Sugar 6.03g; Protein 28.34g

Savory Egg Pizza

Prep time: 5 minutes | Cook time: 10 minutes | Serves: 2

120g shredded mozzarella cheese
7 slices pepperoni, chopped
1 large egg, whisked
¼ teaspoon dried oregano

¼ teaspoon dried parsley
¼ teaspoon garlic powder
¼ teaspoon salt

1. Place mozzarella in a single layer on the bottom of an ungreased baking dish. 2. Scatter pepperoni over cheese, and then pour egg evenly around baking dish, and then sprinkle them with remaining ingredients. 3. Air-fry the food at 165°C for 10 minutes until the cheese is brown and the egg is set. 4. Let the food cool in dish for 5 minutes before serving.
Per Serving: Calories 143; Fat 5.31g; Sodium 838mg; Carbs 2.69g; Fibre 1.1g; Sugar 0.9g; Protein 20.95g

Cinnamon Pecan Granola

Prep time: 10 minutes | Cook time: 7 minutes | Serves: 4 cups

220g shelled pecans, chopped
95g unsweetened coconut flakes
110g slivered almonds

2 tablespoons granular erythritol
1 teaspoon ground cinnamon

1. Mix all ingredients in a bowl, and then transfer the mixture into an ungreased baking dish. 2. Bake the mixture at 160°C for 7 minutes, stirring halfway through cooking. 3. Let the food cool for 10 minutes before serving. 4. This dish can be kept in airtight container at room temperature for up to 5 days.
Per Serving (⅔ cup): Calories 463; Fat 43.16g; Sodium 181mg; Carbs 18.79g; Fibre 7.2g; Sugar 9.8g; Protein 7.26g

Fruit Muffins

Prep time: 15 minutes | Cook time: 15 minutes | Serves: 3

1 ripe banana	2 tablespoons coconut sugar
120ml unsweetened plant-based milk	90g plain flour
1 teaspoon apple cider vinegar	1 teaspoon baking powder
1 teaspoon vanilla extract	½ teaspoon baking soda
2 tablespoons ground flaxseed	110g blueberries

1. Mash the banana with a fork in a bowl; add the plant-based milk, apple cider vinegar, vanilla, flaxseed, and coconut sugar and mix until well combined. Set aside. 2. Whisk the flour, baking powder, and baking soda in a small bowl, and then transfer this mixture to the banana bowl and mix them until just combined. 3. Divide the batter among 6 cupcake molds. 4. Divide the blueberries evenly among the muffins and lightly press them into the batter so that they are at least partially submerged. 5. Bake the molds at 175°C for 16 minutes until the muffins are lightly browned and a toothpick inserted into the centre of a muffin comes out clean. 6. Let the food cool before enjoying.

Per Serving: Calories 254; Fat 4.27g; Sodium 234mg; Carbs 48.44g; Fibre 4.7g; Sugar 16.14g; Protein 6.54g

Quinoa Quiche

Prep time: 5 minutes | Cook time: 20 minutes | Serves: 3

1 (250g) bag frozen mixed vegetables, thawed	20g nutritional yeast
80g quinoa flour	¼ teaspoon granulated garlic
180ml water	¼ teaspoon sea salt
2 tablespoons freshly squeezed lemon juice	Freshly ground black pepper

1. Mix the vegetables, quinoa flour, water, lemon juice, nutritional yeast, granulated garlic, salt, and pepper in a bowl until well combined. 2. Divide the mixture among 6 cupcake molds. 3. Place the filled molds into the air fryer basket, and bake them at 170°C for 20 minutes until the tops are lightly browned and a toothpick inserted into the centre of a muffin comes out clean. 4. Let the food cool slightly before enjoying.

Per Serving: Calories 253; Fat 2.94g; Sodium 935mg; Carbs 42.87g; Fibre 8g; Sugar 3.01g; Protein 13.95g

French Whole-Grain Toast

Prep time: 5 minutes | Cook time: 10 minutes | Serves: 2

1 ripe banana, mashed
40g protein powder
120ml of plant-based milk

2 tablespoons ground flaxseed
4 slices whole-grain bread
Nonstick cooking spray

1. Mix the banana, protein powder, plant-based milk, and flaxseed in a shallow bowl. 2. Dip both sides of each slice of bread into the mixture. 3. Lightly spray the air fryer basket with oil, and place the slices on it in a single layer. Pour any remaining mixture evenly over the bread. 4. Air-fry the slices at 190°C for 10 minutes until golden brown and crispy. 5. Flip the toast over halfway through. 6. Enjoy warm.
Per Serving: Calories 447; Fat 13.1g; Sodium 417mg; Carbs 59.02g; Fibre 12g; Sugar 16.96g; Protein 25.55g

Oat Bowls

Prep time: 5 minutes | Cook time: 15 minutes | Serves: 2

50g of rolled oats
1 apple, cored and diced
4 dates, pitted and diced

½ teaspoon ground cinnamon
180ml unsweetened plant-based milk

1. Combine the oats, apple, dates, and cinnamon in a heatproof bowl. Pour the plant-based milk over the top. 2. Place the bowl in the air fryer basket, and bake the food at 175°C for 12 minutes, stirring them halfway through cooking until the apples are soft. 3. Stir again and let cool slightly before enjoying.
Per Serving: Calories 212; Fat 4.24g; Sodium 46mg; Carbs 49g; Fibre 8.5g; Sugar 23.55g; Protein 9.08g

Yummy Jalapeño Egg Cups

Prep time: 10 minutes | Cook time: 15 minutes | Serves: 4

4 large eggs
½ teaspoon salt
¼ teaspoon ground black pepper
20g chopped pickled jalapeños

50g cream cheese, softened
¼ teaspoon garlic powder
50g shredded sharp Cheddar cheese

1. Beat eggs with salt and pepper in a bowl, and then pour evenly into four ramekins greased with cooking spray. 2. Mix jalapeños, cream cheese, garlic powder, and Cheddar in another bowl. Divide the mixture among the ramekins. 3. Place ramekins in air fryer basket, and then air-fry them at 160°C for 14 minutes until the eggs are set. 4. Serve warm.
Per Serving: Calories 274; Fat 23.37g; Sodium 697mg; Carbs 5.56g; Fibre 0.1g; Sugar 3.14g; Protein 10.81g

Homemade Hash Browns

Prep time: 5 minutes | Cook time: 15 minutes | Serves: 4

630g frozen shredded potatoes, thawed	1 teaspoon no-salt spice blend
2 tablespoons nutritional yeast	1 tablespoon chickpea water

1. Cut 4 pieces of parchment paper, each about 30 cmlong. 2. Mix the potatoes, nutritional yeast, spice blend, and chickpea water in a bowl until well combined. Divide the mixture into 4 equal portions. 3. Place 1 portion onto the middle of a piece of parchment paper. Fold the sides of the paper together and then the top and bottom to create a rectangle about 7.5 by 13cm. 4. Press down on the hash brown to flatten and spread it. 5. Unwrap the parchment paper and use a spatula to carefully transfer the hash brown to the air fryer basket. Do the same with the remaining portions. 6. Air-fry the hash browns at 205°C for 12 minutes until they are lightly browned and crispy, flipping the hash browns halfway through cooking. 7. Enjoy warm.

Per Serving: Calories 123; Fat 0.3g; Sodium 301mg; Carbs 25.72g; Fibre 2.2g; Sugar 1.21g; Protein 5.41g

Tofu Scramble Brunch

Prep time: 10 minutes | Cook time: 15 minutes | Serves: 2

1 medium russet potato, cut into fries or 2.5cm cubes	1 tablespoon nutritional yeast
	½ teaspoon granulated garlic
1 pepper , seeded and cut into 2.5cm strips	½ teaspoon granulated onion
½ (350g) block medium-firm tofu, drained and cubed	¼ teaspoon ground turmeric
	1 tablespoon apple cider vinegar

1. Place the potato and pepper strips in the air fryer basket, and air-fry them at 205°C for 10 minutes. 2. Stir the tofu, nutritional yeast, granulated garlic, onion, turmeric, and apple cider vinegar in a small pan. 3. Add the pan to the air fryer, on a rack above the potatoes and peppers. Continue to fry them at 205°C for an additional 5 minutes until the potatoes are crispy and the tofu is heated through. 4. Remove the food from the air fryer and stir the tofu in the pan. Divide the potatoes and peppers evenly between 2 bowls. Then spoon half the tofu over each bowl. 5. Serve warm.

Per Serving: Calories 273; Fat 4.64g; Sodium 294mg; Carbs 46.21g; Fibre 4.4g; Sugar 7.45g; Protein 14.89g

Special Patties

Prep time: 10 minutes | Cook time: 15 minutes | Serves: 3

50g oat flour
1½ teaspoons no-salt spice blend
½ teaspoon ground sage
1 teaspoon pure maple syrup

½ teaspoon liquid smoke
1 teaspoon balsamic vinegar
6 tablespoons boiling water
Nonstick cooking spray

1. Combine the oat flour, spice blend, sage, maple syrup, liquid smoke, balsamic vinegar, and water in a bowl. 2. Divide the mixture into 6 equal patties and place them on parchment paper. Wet your fingers and flatten the patties to 1 cm thick. 3. Lightly spray the patties with oil and place them in the air fryer basket or on the rack. 4. Grill the patties at 205°C for 12 minutes until the edges of the patties are crispy. 5. Flip the patties over halfway through cooking. 6. Enjoy warm.

Per Serving: Calories 79; Fat 1.69g; Sodium 5mg; Carbs 13.33g; Fibre 1.2g; Sugar 1.75g; Protein 2.58g

Power Tarts

Prep time: 15 minutes | Cook time: 10 minutes | Serves: 2

65g natural peanut butter
1 tablespoon coconut sugar
2 tablespoons unsweetened coconut yogurt

50g oat flour
2 tablespoons blueberry fruit spread

1. Cut 2 pieces of parchment paper, each 20 cm long. On one of the pieces of parchment paper, measure out and draw a 13-by-30 cm rectangle. 2. Combine the peanut butter, coconut sugar, and coconut yogurt in a medium bowl, and then mix in the oat flour to form dough. 3. Place the dough on the blank piece of parchment paper and cover it with the other piece, with the rectangle facing you. Use a rolling pin to evenly roll out the dough to fit in the rectangle. Carefully peel off the top piece of parchment paper. 4. Cut the dough into 4 equal rectangles, each 8 by 13cm. Place 1 tablespoon of the fruit spread on 2 of the rectangles and spread it out evenly. Carefully place the remaining 2 rectangles on top of the fruit spread and gently press on the edges with a fork to seal them. 5. Place the tarts in the air fryer basket, and bake them at 175°C for 8 minutes. 6. Enjoy warm.

Per Serving: Calories 311; Fat 14.64g; Sodium 215mg; Carbs 34.46g; Fibre 3.7g; Sugar 7.85g; Protein 13.24g

Onion Avocado Bagels

Prep time: 10 minutes | Cook time: 10 minutes | Serves: 2

80g plain flour, plus more as needed	1 ripe avocado
½ teaspoon active dry yeast	1 tablespoon freshly squeezed lemon juice
80g unsweetened coconut yogurt	2 tablespoons finely chopped red onion
8 cherry or grape tomatoes	Freshly ground black pepper

1. Combine the flour, yeast, and coconut yogurt in a bowl. Knead into smooth dough. If the dough is too sticky, add more flour as necessary. 2. Divide the dough into 2 equal balls. Roll each ball into a 23 cm-long rope. Then form a ring with each rope and press the ends together to connect them. 3. Fill a medium bowl with hot (but not boiling) water. Soak the bagels in the water for 1 minute. Then shake off the excess water and place them in the air fryer basket to rise for 15 minutes. 4. Bake the bagels at 205°C for 10 minutes, flipping them and adding the tomatoes to the air fryer basket halfway through cooking. 5. Cut the avocado in half and carefully remove the pit. Scoop the avocado out into a small bowl and mash it with a fork. Mix in the lemon juice and red onion. 6. Let the bagels cool slightly before cutting them in half. Divide the avocado mixture among the 4 bagel halves. Top each bagel half with 2 baked tomatoes and season with pepper.
Per Serving: Calories 351; Fat 15.39g; Sodium 50mg; Carbs 49.17g; Fibre 9.5g; Sugar 6.63g; Protein 7.52g

Curry Samosa Rolls

Prep time: 15 minutes | Cook time: 15 minutes | Serves: 4

100g frozen peas, thawed	1 teaspoon curry powder
4 spring onions, both white and green parts, finely sliced	25g chickpea flour
	1 tablespoon tahini
70g grated sweet potato	80ml water
2 tablespoons freshly squeezed lemon juice	8 (15cm) rice paper wrappers
1 teaspoon ground ginger	

1. Combine the peas, spring onions, sweet potato, lemon juice, ginger, curry powder, and chickpea flour in a bowl. 2. Mix the tahini and water in a small bowl until well combined. Pour the mixture onto a plate. 3. Dip both sides of a rice paper wrapper into the tahini mixture. When the wrapper starts to soften up, transfer it to another plate. 4. Spoon about ⅓ cup of the filling onto the wrapper and wrap it up tightly, burrito style. 5. Place the roll in the air fryer basket with seam-side down, and repeat this process with the remaining ingredients to form 7 more rolls. 6. Bake the rolls at 175°C for 15 minutes or until the wrappers are lightly browned and crispy. 7. Flip the rolls over halfway through cooking. 8. Serve warm.
Per Serving: Calories 165; Fat 3.04g; Sodium 101mg; Carbs 30.23g; Fibre 4g; Sugar 1.29g; Protein 4.89g

Glazed Apple Fritters

Prep time: 10 minutes | Cook time: 20 minutes | Serves: 8

For Fritters
Oil spray (hand-pumped)
2 medium apples, peeled, cored, and chopped
150g plain flour
70g granulated sugar
2 teaspoons baking powder

1 teaspoon pumpkin pie spice
⅛ teaspoon sea salt
120ml apple juice
1 large egg

For Glaze
50g cream cheese
2 tablespoons salted butter, at room temperature

125g icing sugar

1. Preheat the air fryer to 175°C on Air Fry mode for 5 minutes. 2. Place parchment paper on the baking tray and spray generously with oil. 3. Press the chopped apple between paper towels to dry it out. 4. Mix the flour, sugar, baking powder, pumpkin pie spice, and salt in a bowl, when combined, toss in the apple. 5. Mix the apple juice and egg in a small bowl until blended; add the mixture to the flour mixture and mix them well. 6. Drop the fritters onto the baking sheet using a ¼-cup scoop and lightly spray them with the oil. 7. Air-fry the fritters in the preheated air fryer for 10 minutes, turning the fritters over and spraying them with oil halfway through cooking. 8. Stir the cream cheese, butter, and icing sugar in a separate bowl until smooth. 9. Transfer the cooked fritters to a rack and spread with the glaze while hot. 10. Serve.

Per Serving: Calories 213; Fat 4.82g; Sodium 89mg; Carbs 40.59g; Fibre 1.7g; Sugar 22.81g; Protein 3.03g

Apple-Cinnamon Cookies

Prep time: 5 minutes | Cook time: 10 minutes | Serves: 3

1 medium apple
100g oat flour
2 tablespoons pure maple syrup

65g natural peanut butter
50g raisins
½ teaspoon ground cinnamon

1. Carefully grate each side of the apple down to the core. Place the grated apple in a medium bowl, and then mix them with the oat flour, maple syrup, peanut butter, raisins and cinnamon. 2. Scoop out 2-tablespoon balls of dough onto parchment paper. 3. Transfer the cookies to the air fryer basket and bake them at 175°C for 9 minutes until the edges of the cookies start to brown. 4. Enjoy warm.

Per Serving: Calories 332; Fat 11.44g; Sodium 138mg; Carbs 49.05g; Fibre 5.2g; Sugar 16.92g; Protein 11.48g

Golden Pancake

Prep time: 10 minutes | Cook time: 20 minutes | Serves: 2

80ml whole milk, room temperature	⅛ teaspoon sea salt
2 large eggs, room temperature	⅛ teaspoon ground cinnamon
1 tablespoon granulated sugar	40g plain flour
1 teaspoon orange zest	1 tablespoon unsalted butter
1 teaspoon pure vanilla extract	Maple syrup, for serving

1. Preheat the air fryer at 175°C for 5 minutes on Bake mode. 2. Mix up the milk, eggs, sugar, orange zest, vanilla, salt, and cinnamon in a large bowl, and then mix in the flour until smooth. 3. Melt the butter in a cake pan in the air fryer for 2 minutes, and then pour in the batter. 4. Bake the batter for 15 minutes until puffy and golden. 5. Serve the food with a drizzle of maple syrup.

Per Serving: Calories 224; Fat 9.81g; Sodium 184mg; Carbs 26.24g; Fibre 0.6g; Sugar 9.72g; Protein 6.28g

Glory Muffins

Prep time: 10 minutes | Cook time: 25 minutes | Serves: 6

Oil spray (hand-pumped)	120g carrot, finely shredded
35g raisins	1 small apple, peeled, cored, and shredded
125g whole-wheat flour	30g shredded, sweetened coconut
100g packed dark brown sugar	2 large eggs
1 teaspoon baking soda	60ml rapeseed oil
1¼ teaspoons pumpkin pie spice	Juice and zest of ½ orange
¼ teaspoon sea salt	

1. Preheat the air fryer at 175°C for 5 minutes on Bake mode. 2. Lightly spray 6 muffin cups with the oil. 3. In a small bowl, cover the raisins with hot water and set aside. 4. Whisk the flour, brown sugar, baking soda, pumpkin pie spice, salt, carrot, apple, and coconut in a large bowl. 5. Beat the eggs with the oil, orange juice, and orange zest in a small bowl. 6. Drain the raisins, squeezing out as much water as possible. 7. Add the wet ingredients and raisins to the dry ingredients and mix until the batter is just combined. Divide the batter among the muffin cups. 8. Bake the muffins for 25 minutes until a knife inserted in the centre comes out clean. 9. When done, let the food cool for a while and then enjoy.

Per Serving: Calories 245; Fat 12.54g; Sodium 336mg; Carbs 31.53g; Fibre 3.8g; Sugar 14.07g; Protein 3.99g

Chapter 2 Vegetable and Sides Recipes

Broccoli Salad

Prep time: 10 minutes | Cook time: 5 minutes | Serves: 2

1 large bunch broccoli, cut into bite-sized florets
1 tablespoon olive oil
1 tablespoon balsamic vinegar
2 tablespoons water
2 tablespoons raisins

2 tablespoons roasted, salted pepitas
2 tablespoons diced peeled red onion
60g vegan mayonnaise
⅛ teaspoon ground black pepper

1. Preheat the air fryer at 175°C for 3 minutes. 2. Combine the florets, olive oil, and balsamic vinegar in a bowl. 3. Pour the water in a suitable baking pan, and add the florets; air-fry the florets for 5 minutes. 4. Toss the cooked florets with raisins, pepitas, onion, mayonnaise, and black pepper in a bowl. 5. Cover the bowl, and refrigerate the dish until ready to enjoy.

Per Serving: Calories 293; Fat 20.17g; Sodium 375mg; Carbs 14.31g; Fibre 8.6g; Sugar 4.13g; Protein 14.16g

Crispy Tofu & Sweet Potato

Prep time: 15 minutes | Cook time: 16 minutes | Serves: 2

½ small yellow onion, peeled and sliced
35g small-diced peeled sweet potato
1 teaspoon avocado oil
200g extra-firm tofu, cut into ½cm cubes
½ teaspoon smoked paprika

½ teaspoon chili powder
¼ teaspoon salt
2 teaspoons lime zest
185g cooked quinoa
2 lime wedges

1. Preheat the air fryer at 175°C for 3 minutes. 2. Combine the onion, sweet potato, and avocado oil in a bowl; toss the tofu cubes with paprika, chili powder, and salt in another bowl. 3. Arrange the onion mixture into the air fryer basket, and then air-fry them for 16 minutes, stirring in the tofu mixture halfway through. 4. Stir lime zest into cooked quinoa, then portion out quinoa into two serving bowls. 5. Evenly distribute cooked tofu mixture over quinoa. Squeeze one lime wedge over each bowl. Serve immediately.

Per Serving: Calories 264; Fat 10.96g; Sodium 329mg; Carbs 29.95g; Fibre 4.9g; Sugar 3.06g; Protein 16.3g

Vegan Sandwiches

Prep time: 10 minutes | Cook time: 10 minutes | Serves: 2

2 tablespoons balsamic vinegar

4 slices gluten-free sandwich bread

50g vegan mozzarella shreds

2 medium Roma tomatoes, sliced

8 fresh basil leaves

2 tablespoons olive oil

1. Preheat the air fryer at 175°C for 3 minutes. 2. Drizzle balsamic vinegar on bottom bread slices, and place the mozzarella, tomatoes, and basil leaves on them. 3. Lightly brush the bread slices with olive oil, and then place them in the air fryer basket. 4. Air-fry the sandwiches for 5 minutes, flipping them halfway through. You can cook the sandwiches in batches. 5. Serve warm.

Per Serving: Calories 440; Fat 22.6g; Sodium 511mg; Carbs 41.19g; Fibre 6.3g; Sugar 8.67g; Protein 17.93g

Cheese Bean Taquitos

Prep time: 10 minutes | Cook time: 15 minutes | Serves: 5

240g vegetarian refried beans

200g dairy-free Cheddar shreds

15 (15cm) soft corn tortillas

1. Preheat the air fryer at 175°C for 3 minutes. 2. Spread the beans and Cheddar shreds on each corn tortilla. Roll each tortilla tightly and place seam side down on a large serving platter. 3. Arrange the tortillas into the air fryer basket with seam side down, and then air-fry them for 4 minutes. You can cook them in batches. 4. Serve warm.

Per Serving: Calories 378; Fat 20.05g; Sodium 373mg; Carbs 34.16g; Fibre 5.1g; Sugar 1.02g; Protein 17.14g

Barbecue Pulled Jackfruit

Prep time: 5 minutes | Cook time: 10 minutes | Serves: 2

1 (500g) can green jackfruit in brine, drained and chopped

160ml barbecue sauce, divided

1. Preheat the air fryer at 190°C for 3 minutes. 2. Toss jackfruit with 80 ml barbecue sauce in a medium bowl. 3. Lightly grease the air fryer basket with cooking oil, and then arrange the jackfruit into the air fryer basket. 4. Air-fry the jackfruit for 10 minutes, tossing them halfway through. 5. Transfer the jackfruit to a separate bowl and add the remaining sauce to it; pull apart jackfruit to resemble pulled pork. Serve warm.

Per Serving: Calories 241; Fat 1.17g; Sodium 1667mg; Carbs 54.54g; Fibre 9.1g; Sugar 33.54g; Protein 8.07g

Marinated Tofu Cubes

Prep time: 15 minutes | Cook time: 20 minutes | Serves: 4

For Marinade

80ml vegetable stock

2 tablespoons tomato sauce

1 tablespoon nutritional yeast

1 teaspoon Italian seasoning

1 teaspoon granulated sugar

½ teaspoon fennel seeds

½ teaspoon garlic powder

¼ teaspoon salt

¼ teaspoon ground black pepper

350g firm tofu, cut into 2 cm cubes

For Breading

65g plain gluten-free bread crumbs

2 teaspoons nutritional yeast

1 teaspoon Italian seasoning

½ teaspoon salt

For Dip

240ml marinara sauce, heated

1. Combine all of the marinade ingredients in a large bowl to coat the tofu cubes well. 2. Refrigerate the tofu cubes for 30 minutes, tossing them once after 15 minutes. 3. Preheat the air fryer at 175°C for 3 minutes. 4. Mix up all of the breading ingredients in a shallow dish. 5. Dredge the marinated tofu cubes in bread crumb mixture. 6. Lightly grease the air fryer basket with cooking oil, and then place the tofu cubes in it. 7. Air-fry the tofu cubes for 10 minutes, flipping them and brushing them with additional cooking oil halfway through. You can cook the tofu cubes in batches. 8. Serve warm with marinara dip on the side.

Per Serving: Calories 442; Fat 27.84g; Sodium 1482mg; Carbs 26.85g; Fibre 5.6g; Sugar 5.45g; Protein 21.27g

Chili Dogs

Prep time: 5 minutes | Cook time: 5 minutes | Serves: 4

4 vegan hot dogs

4 gluten-free hot dog buns

70g leftover vegetarian chili, warmed

2 tablespoons Dijon mustard

1. Preheat the air fryer to 205°C for 3 minutes. 2. Place the hot dogs in the air fryer basket and air-fry them for 4 minutes. 3. Transfer hot dogs to hot dog buns, and place them back to the basket, and cook for 1 minute. 4. Transfer hot dogs in buns to a large plate and garnish with warmed chili and mustard. Serve warm.

Per Serving: Calories 203; Fat 2.42g; Sodium 1596mg; Carbs 43.23g; Fibre 4.1g; Sugar 2.02g; Protein 6.25g

Stuffed Potatoes with Dressing

Prep time: 10 minutes | Cook time: 50 minutes | Serves: 2

For Green Goddess Dressing

60g vegan sour cream

½ medium avocado, peeled, pitted, and diced

2 tablespoons plain unsweetened almond milk

2 teaspoons lemon juice

½ teaspoon lemon zest

For Potatoes

2 teaspoons olive oil

2 large russet potatoes, scrubbed and perforated with a fork

½ teaspoon salt

1 green onion, roughly chopped

2 cloves garlic, peeled and quartered

10g chopped fresh parsley

½ teaspoon salt

¼ teaspoon ground black pepper

¼ teaspoon ground black pepper

90g steamed broccoli florets

100g canned cannellini beans, drained and rinsed

1. Add all of the dressing ingredients to a food processor, and pulse them until smooth. Transfer the dressing to a bowl, cover the bowl and then refrigerate it until ready to use. 2. Preheat the air fryer at 205°C for 3 minutes. 3. Coat the potatoes with olive oil and season them with salt and pepper. 4. Place the potatoes in the air fryer basket, and then air-fry them for 45 minutes. 5. After 30 minutes of cooking time, flip the potatoes and then resume cooking them. 6. Transfer cooked potatoes to a cutting board to rest 5 minutes until cool enough to handle. Slice each potato lengthwise. Pinch ends of each potato together to open up each slice. 7. Stuff broccoli and beans into potatoes and place potatoes back into the air fryer basket, and air-fry them for 3 minutes more. 8. Transfer stuffed potatoes to a large serving plate. Pour Green Goddess Dressing over potatoes and serve warm.

Per Serving: Calories 582; Fat 24.64g; Sodium 1263mg; Carbs 82.63g; Fibre 12.2g; Sugar 5.71g; Protein 15.18g

Broccoli Salad

Prep time: 10 minutes | Cook time: 10 minutes | Serves: 2

270g fresh broccoli florets

2 tablespoons salted butter, melted

20g sliced almonds

½ medium lemon

1. Arrange the broccoli into a suitable baking dish, and the pour the butter over the top; toss in the almonds. 2. Air-fry the food at 195°C for 7 minutes, stirring them halfway through. 3. When the cooking time is up, zest lemon onto broccoli and squeeze juice into the dish. Toss and enjoy.

Per Serving: Calories 84; Fat 8.02g; Sodium 82mg; Carbs 2.58g; Fibre 1.7g; Sugar 0.54g; Protein 2.06g

Homemade Giant Nachos

Prep time: 10 minutes | Cook time: 10 minutes | Serves: 2

2 tablespoons vegan sour cream
½ teaspoon chili powder
½ teaspoon + ⅛ teaspoon salt, divided
2 (15cm) soft corn tortillas
2 teaspoons avocado oil
130g vegetarian refried beans

25g vegan Cheddar cheese shreds
2 tablespoons sliced black olives
15g shredded iceberg lettuce
1 large Roma tomato, seeded and diced
2 lime wedges

1. Preheat the air fryer at 205°C for 3 minutes. 2. Combine the sour cream, chili powder, and ⅛ teaspoon salt in a small bowl. 3. Brush tortillas with oil and sprinkle one side with remaining salt. 4. Place one tortilla in the air fryer basket, and air-fry it in the preheated air fryer for 3 minutes. Set aside and do the same with second tortilla. 5. Add refried beans and Cheddar cheese shreds to tortillas. Place one tortilla in air fryer basket and cook 2 minutes. Set aside and repeat with second tortilla. 6. Transfer tortillas to two serving plates and top with black olives, lettuce, and tomatoes. Dollop sour cream mixture on each and serve warm with lime wedges on the side for spritzing.
Per Serving: Calories 208; Fat 10.38g; Sodium 1004mg; Carbs 24.91g; Fibre 4.2g; Sugar 6.08g; Protein 7.33g

Potato–Stuffed Peppers

Prep time: 15 minutes | Cook time: 60 minutes | Serves: 4

2 teaspoons olive oil
2 large russet potatoes, scrubbed and perforated with a fork
2 (75g) meatless Italian sausages, smoked, diced into ½ cmcubes
2 tablespoons plain unsweetened almond milk
1 teaspoon olive oil

1 tablespoon Italian seasoning
¼ teaspoon salt
¼ teaspoon ground black pepper
40g canned corn kernels, drained
60g vegan mozzarella shreds
4 medium green peppers, tops and insides discarded

1. Preheat the air fryer at 205°Cfor 3 minutes. 2. Rub the potatoes with olive oil and place them in the air fryer basket. 3. Air-fry the potatoes for 30 minutes; flip them and resume cooking them for 15 minutes more. 4. Transfer cooked potatoes to a cutting board and let rest 5 minutes until cool enough to handle. Scoop out cooled potato into a medium bowl. Discard the skins. 5. Add sausage to the air fryer basket and air-fry for 2 minutes. 6. Combine potatoes with almond milk, olive oil, Italian seasoning, salt, and black pepper. Toss in cooked Italian sausage, corn, and mozzarella. 7. Stuff peppers with potato mixture. Add peppers to the air fryer basket and air-fry for 10 minutes. 8. Transfer cooked peppers to a large plate and serve warm.
Per Serving: Calories 345; Fat 14.18g; Sodium 612mg; Carbs 44.96g; Fibre 5.1g; Sugar 4.66g; Protein 13.36g

Avocado Tacos

Prep time: 10 minutes | Cook time: 10 minutes | Serves: 3

For Salsa
2 medium Roma tomatoes, seeded and diced
40g finely diced peeled red onion
1 tablespoon fresh lime juice

1 teaspoon lime zest
10g chopped fresh coriander
1 teaspoon salt

For Avocado Fries
Vegan egg substitute equaling 1 large egg
2 tablespoons plain unsweetened almond milk
100g plain gluten-free bread crumbs

1 large avocado, peeled, pitted, and sliced into 6 "fries"

For Tacos
6 (15cm) gluten-free flour tortillas
80g coleslaw mix

1 batch Sriracha Mayonnaise

1. Combine all of the salsa ingredients in a small bowl, cover the bowl and refrigerate the salsa until ready to use. 2. Preheat the air fryer at 190°C for 3 minutes. 3. Whisk together egg substitute and almond milk in a small bowl. Add bread crumbs to a separate shallow dish. 4. Dip avocado slices in egg mixture. Dredge them in bread crumbs. 5. Lightly grease the air fryer basket with cooking oil, and place the avocado slices into it. 6. Air-fry the avocado slices for 5 minutes. Transfer cooked avocado slices to a large serving plate. You can cook the avocado slices in batches. 7. Add two fried avocado fries to each tortilla. Top with coleslaw mix, salsa, and Sriracha Mayonnaise. Serve.

Per Serving: Calories 684; Fat 27.87g; Sodium 1832mg; Carbs 93.09g; Fibre 10.9g; Sugar 11.01g; Protein 18.21g

---

Cauliflower Steak

Prep time: 5 minutes | Cook time: 10 minutes | Serves: 4

1 medium head cauliflower
60ml hot sauce
2 tablespoons salted butter, melted

60g blue cheese crumbles
60ml full-fat ranch dressing

1. Remove the cauliflower leaves, and slice the head in 1 cm-thick slices. 2. Mix hot sauce and butter in a small bowl, and then brush the cauliflower with the mixture. 3. Place each cauliflower steaks into the air fryer basket, and then air-fry them at 205°C for 7 minutes until the edges begin turning dark and caramelized. 4. Sprinkle the steaks with crumbled blue cheese and drizzle with ranch dressing, then enjoy.

Per Serving: Calories 91; Fat 6.14g; Sodium 614mg; Carbs 7.49g; Fibre 1.4g; Sugar 2.38g; Protein 2.8g

Lemon Aubergine Dip

Prep time: 5 minutes | Cook time: 30 minutes | Serves: 4

2½ teaspoons olive oil, divided
1 medium aubergine, halved lengthwise
2 teaspoons pine nuts
60g tahini
1 tablespoon lemon juice

2 cloves garlic, peeled and minced
⅛ teaspoon ground cumin
¼ teaspoon salt
⅛ teaspoon ground black pepper
1 tablespoon chopped fresh parsley

1. Preheat the air fryer at 190°C for 3 minutes. 2. Rub the aubergine halves with 2 teaspoons of olive oil. Pierce aubergine flesh three times per half with a fork. 3. Place aubergine flat side down in the air fryer basket. Air-fry the aubergine flat for 25 minutes. 4. Transfer cooked aubergine to a cutting board and let sit 5 minutes until cool enough to handle. 5. Add pine nuts to the air fryer basket, and air-fry them for 2 minutes, shaking every 30 seconds to ensure they don't burn. Set aside in a small bowl. 6. Transfer the aubergine flesh to a food processor bowl; add the tahini, lemon juice, garlic, cumin, salt, and pepper, and pulse them well. 7. Transfer dip to a medium bowl. Garnish with roasted pine nuts, chopped parsley, and remaining olive oil.

Per Serving: Calories 149; Fat 10.71g; Sodium 166mg; Carbs 12.33g; Fibre 5.7g; Sugar 5.08g; Protein 4.25g

Mini Mushroom–Onion Pizzas

Prep time: 5 minutes | Cook time: 16 minutes | Serves: 4

2 teaspoons + 2 tablespoons olive oil, divided
40g small-diced peeled yellow onion
50g small-diced white mushrooms
120ml marinara sauce

1 small aubergine, sliced into 8 (1cm) circles
1 teaspoon salt
120g shredded mozzarella
10g chopped fresh basil

1. Heat 2 teaspoons of olive oil in a frying pan over medium heat for 30 seconds; add the onion and mushrooms, and cook them for 5 minutes until onions are translucent; add marinara sauce and stir. 2. Preheat the air fryer at 190°C for 3 minutes. 3. Coat the aubergine circles with the remaining olive oil on both sides. Lay circles on a large plate and season tops evenly with salt. Top with marinara sauce mixture, followed by shredded mozzarella. 4. Place the aubergine pizzas in the air fryer basket, and air-fry them for 5 minutes. You can cook the pizzas in batches. 5. Garnish the pizzas with chopped basil and serve warm.

Per Serving: Calories 111; Fat 3.15g; Sodium 1024mg; Carbs 11.74g; Fibre 5.3g; Sugar 6.8g; Protein 10.94g

Breaded White Mushrooms

Prep time: 10 minutes | Cook time: 10 minutes | Serves: 2

75g gluten-free crispy rice cereal	1 tablespoon Dijon mustard
1 teaspoon Italian seasoning	1 tablespoon vegan mayonnaise
1 teaspoon nutritional yeast	60ml plain unsweetened almond milk
⅛ teaspoon salt	200g whole white mushrooms

1. Add the cereal, Italian seasoning, nutritional yeast, and salt to a food processor, and then pulse them until a bread crumb consistency forms. 2. Whisk the mustard, mayonnaise, and almond milk in a bowl. 3. Preheat the air fryer at 175°C for 3 minutes. 4. Dip mushrooms in wet mixture, and shake off any excess. Dredge them in dry mixture, and shake off any excess. 5. Lightly grease the air fryer basket with cooking oil, and then arrange the mushrooms into the air fryer basket. 6. Air-fry the mushrooms for 7 minutes, tossing them halfway through. 7. Serve warm.

Per Serving: Calories 197; Fat 4.27g; Sodium 700mg; Carbs 35.67g; Fibre 4.2g; Sugar 6.73g; Protein 6.51g

Quinoa Patties

Prep time: 10 minutes | Cook time: 10 minutes | Serves: 4

80ml water	2 tablespoons finely chopped peeled yellow onion
1 tablespoon + ½ teaspoon olive oil, divided	2 tablespoons chopped fresh coriander
½ teaspoon ground cumin	1 teaspoon chili powder
½ teaspoon garlic salt	½ teaspoon salt
55g uncooked quinoa	2 tablespoons creamy tree nut cheese
180g canned tri-bean blend, drained and rinsed	

1. Add water, 1 tablespoon of olive oil, cumin, garlic, and salt to the saucepan, and boil them over high heat. Turn off the heat and stir in the quinoa, then cover the saucepan and let them rest for 5 minutes. 2. Preheat the air fryer to 175°C for 3 minutes. 3. Mash the beans in a medium bowl; add the cooked quinoa, onion, coriander, chili powder, salt, and tree nut cheese, and mix them well. 4. Form the mixture into four patties. 5. Lightly grease the air fryer basket with cooking oil, and then arrange the patties into the air fryer basket. 6. Air-fry the patties for 6 minutes, brushing them with the remaining olive oil halfway through. 7. Serve warm.

Per Serving: Calories 146; Fat 8.16g; Sodium 345mg; Carbs 15.27g; Fibre 2.7g; Sugar 2.71g; Protein 3.58g

Cheese Vegetarian Lasagna

Prep time: 15 minutes | Cook time: 25 minutes | Serves: 4

1 medium courgette , diced
50g diced white mushrooms
40g diced peeled yellow onion
240ml marinara sauce
240g ricotta cheese
35g grated Parmesan cheese

1 large egg
2 teaspoons Italian seasoning
½ teaspoon salt, divided
5 sheets gluten-free air fryer-ready lasagna noodles
120g grated mozzarella cheese

1. Cook the courgette, mushrooms, and onion in a frying pan over medium-high heat for 4 minutes until they are tender. 2. Stir in the marinara sauce, turn the heat to high and then boil them; when boiled, reduce the heat to medium and simmer the food for 3 minutes. 3. Preheat the air fryer at 190°C for 3 minutes. 4. Combine ricotta cheese, Parmesan cheese, egg, Italian seasoning, and salt in a bowl. 5. Prepare four cake barrels, and divide the vegetable mixture among them. Place a layer of lasagna noodles on top, breaking apart noodles first to fit pan. Top with one-third ricotta mixture, followed by one-fourth mozzarella. Repeat two more times with vegetables, noodles, ricotta, and mozzarella. 6. Cover lasagna with aluminum foil and place barrel in the air fryer basket. 7. Air-fry the food for 15 minutes; after 12 minutes of cooking time, remove the foil and resume cooking them. 8. Allow the dish to rest for 10 minutes before serving.
Per Serving: Calories 248; Fat 12.25g; Sodium 1288mg; Carbs 14.06g; Fibre 2.1g; Sugar 3.81g; Protein 21.07g

Pineapple Salsa

Prep time: 5 minutes | Cook time: 10 minutes | Serves: 2-4

For Pineapple
165g (½cm) cubes fresh pineapple
⅛ teaspoon salt

¼ teaspoon olive oil
Juice of 1 lime wedge

For Salsa
1 large jalapeño, seeded and diced
2 medium Roma tomatoes, seeded and diced
1 small avocado, peeled, pitted, and diced
40g diced peeled red onion
1 tablespoon chopped fresh coriander

2 cloves garlic, peeled and minced
½ teaspoon granulated sugar
Juice of ½ lime
¼ teaspoon salt

1. Preheat the air fryer at 205°C for 3 minutes. 2. Toss the pineapple with salt, olive oil, and lime juice in a bowl. 3. Lightly grease the air fryer basket with cooking oil, and then arrange the pineapple into the air fryer basket. 4. Air-fry the pineapple for 8 minutes, tossing them halfway through. 5. Transfer pineapple to a medium bowl. Add Salsa ingredients and toss. Refrigerate up to two days until ready to serve.
Per Serving: Calories 146; Fat 7.86g; Sodium 232mg; Carbs 20.41g; Fibre 5g; Sugar 12.44g; Protein 2.28g

Avocado Rice Bowls

Prep time: 5 minutes | Cook time: 5 minutes | Serves: 4

240g vegan sour cream	240g canned black beans, drained and rinsed
2 tablespoons plain unsweetened almond milk	165g canned corn kernels, drained
1 teaspoon ground cumin	1 teaspoon olive oil
1 teaspoon chili powder	800g cooked brown rice
⅛ teaspoon cayenne pepper	3 medium Roma tomatoes, diced
½ teaspoon salt	1 medium avocado, peeled, pitted, and diced

1. Combine sour cream, almond milk, cumin, chili powder, cayenne pepper, and salt in a bowl, and then cover the bowl and refrigerate the mixture until ready to use. 2. Preheat the air fryer to 175°C for 3 minutes. 3. Toss beans and corn with olive oil in another bowl. 4. Place mixture in the air fryer basket, and air-fry them for 5 minutes. 5. Distribute brown rice among four serving bowls. Top the dish with black bean and corn mixture, tomatoes, and avocado. Drizzle sour cream mixture over top of each bowl and serve immediately.

Per Serving: Calories 541; Fat 21.98g; Sodium 471mg; Carbs 75.2g; Fibre 13.8g; Sugar 5.13g; Protein 15.49g

Cheese Courgette Boats

Prep time: 15 minutes | Cook time: 20 minutes | Serves: 2

2 medium courgette	¼ teaspoon dried oregano
1 tablespoon avocado oil	¼ teaspoon garlic powder
60ml low-carb, no-sugar-added pasta sauce	½ teaspoon dried parsley
60g full-fat ricotta cheese	2 tablespoons grated vegetarian Parmesan cheese
30g shredded mozzarella cheese	

1. Cut off 2.5cm from the top and bottom of each courgette. 2. Slice courgette in half lengthwise and use a spoon to scoop out a bit of the inside, making room for filling; brush them with oil and spoon 2 tablespoons pasta sauce into each shell. 3. Mix ricotta, mozzarella, oregano, garlic powder, and parsley in a bowl. 4. Spoon the mixture into each courgette shell. Place stuffed courgette shells into the air fryer basket. 5. Air-fry the courgette shells at 175°Cfor 20 minutes. 6. Top the shells with Parmesan and enjoy.

Per Serving: Calories 169; Fat 11.09g; Sodium 207mg; Carbs 8.23g; Fibre 2.1g; Sugar 2.79g; Protein 10.37g

Vegetable Quesadilla

Prep time: 10 minutes | Cook time: 5 minutes | Serves: 2

1 tablespoon coconut oil
½ medium green pepper , seeded and chopped
40g diced red onion
25g chopped white mushrooms
4 flatbread dough tortillas

65g shredded pepper jack cheese
½ medium avocado, peeled, pitted, and mashed
60g full-fat sour cream
75g mild salsa

1. Heat the coconut oil in the frying pan over medium heat; add the pepper, onion, and mushrooms, and sauté them for 3 to 5 minutes until peppers begin to soften. 2. Place two tortillas on a work surface and sprinkle each with half of cheese. Top them with sautéed veggies, sprinkle with remaining cheese, and place remaining two tortillas on top. 3. Place quesadillas in the air fryer basket, and then air-fry them at 205°C for 5 minutes, flipping them halfway through. 4. Serve warm with avocado, sour cream, and salsa.

Per Serving: Calories 623; Fat 33.2g; Sodium 1207mg; Carbs 62.17g; Fibre 6.8g; Sugar 6.51g; Protein 21.43g

Stuffed Aubergine

Prep time: 15 minutes | Cook time: 20 minutes | Serves: 2

1 large aubergine
2 tablespoons unsalted butter
¼ medium yellow onion, diced
45g chopped artichoke hearts

30g fresh spinach
2 tablespoons diced red pepper
120g crumbled feta

1. Slice aubergine in half lengthwise and scoop out flesh, leaving enough inside for shell to remain intact. Take aubergine that was scooped out, chop it, and set aside. 2. Sauté the butter and onions in the frying pan over medium heat for 3 to 5 minutes until the onions begin to soften; add the chopped aubergine, artichokes, spinach, and pepper, and cook them for 5 minutes more until peppers soften and spinach wilts. 3. Turn off the heat and gently fold in the feta. 4. Place filling into each aubergine shell and place into the air fryer basket. 5. Air-fry them at 160°C for 20 minutes until tender. 6. Serve warm.

Per Serving: Calories 259; Fat 16.32g; Sodium 386mg; Carbs 22.16g; Fibre 10.1g; Sugar 12.44g; Protein 9.81g

Spinach & Artichoke Casserole

Prep time: 15 minutes | Cook time: 15 minutes | Serves: 4

1 tablespoon salted butter, melted
40g diced yellow onion
200g full-fat cream cheese, softened
80g full-fat mayonnaise
80g full-fat sour cream

20g chopped pickled jalapeños
60g fresh spinach, chopped
180g cauliflower florets, chopped
170g artichoke hearts, chopped

1. Mix the butter, onion, cream cheese, mayonnaise, and sour cream in a large bowl; fold in jalapeños, spinach, cauliflower, and artichokes. 2. Transfer the mixture to a round baking dish and cover them with foil. 3. Air-fry the food at 190°C for 15 minutes. 4. When there are 2 minutes left, remove the foil to brown the top. 5. When done, serve and enjoy.

Per Serving: Calories 278; Fat 18.07g; Sodium 467mg; Carbs 21.33g; Fibre 4.4g; Sugar 7.95g; Protein 10.42g

Cheese Zoodle

Prep time: 10 minutes | Cook time: 10 minutes | Serves: 4

2 tablespoons salted butter
40g diced white onion
½ teaspoon minced garlic
120g heavy whipping cream

50g full-fat cream cheese
100g shredded sharp Cheddar cheese
2 medium courgette , spiralized

1. Melt the butter in a saucepan over medium heat; add the onion and sauté for 1 to 3 minutes until it begins to soften; add the garlic and sauté them for 30 seconds, then pour in cream and add cream cheese. 2. Turn off the heat and stir in the Cheddar; add the courgette and toss in the sauce, then put into a round baking dish. Cover the dish with foil. 3. Air-fry the food at 190°C for 8 minutes. 4. After 6 minutes of cooking time, remove the foil to brown the top. 5. When done, stir and serve.

Per Serving: Calories 263; Fat 23.24g; Sodium 323mg; Carbs 4.33g; Fibre 0.3g; Sugar 1.49g; Protein 9.75g

Roasted Lemon Cauliflower

Prep time: 5 minutes | Cook time: 15 minutes | Serves: 4

1 medium head cauliflower
2 tablespoons salted butter, melted
1 medium lemon

½ teaspoon garlic powder
1 teaspoon dried parsley

1. Remove the leaves from the head of cauliflower and brush it with melted butter. 2. Cut the lemon in half and zest one half onto the cauliflower. Squeeze the juice of the zested lemon half and pour it over the cauliflower. 3. Sprinkle them with garlic powder and parsley. 4. Place the cauliflower head in the air fryer basket, and then roast them at 175°C for 15 minutes until fork tender. 5. Squeeze juice from other lemon half over cauliflower and serve immediately.

Per Serving: Calories 54; Fat 4.03g; Sodium 51mg; Carbs 4.43g; Fibre 1.4g; Sugar 1.58g; Protein 1.43g

Cauliflower Pizza Crust

Prep time: 15 minutes | Cook time: 15 minutes | Serves: 2

1 (300g) steamer bag cauliflower
50g shredded sharp Cheddar cheese
1 large egg

2 tablespoons blanched finely ground almond flour
1 teaspoon Italian blend seasoning

1. Cook the cauliflower according to package instructions. 2. Remove excess water and place the cauliflower in a large bowl. 3. Add cheese, egg, almond flour, and Italian seasoning to the bowl and mix well. 4. Line the air fryer basket with parchment paper; press the cauliflower into round circle and then place them in the air fryer basket. 5. Air-fry the food at 180°C for 11 minutes, flipping them halfway through. 6. Add preferred toppings to pizza. Place them back into air fryer basket and cook an additional 4 minutes or until fully cooked and golden. 7. Serve immediately.

Per Serving: Calories 361; Fat 26.69g; Sodium 526mg; Carbs 12.51g; Fibre 4.5g; Sugar 4.03g; Protein 20.38g

Mini Portobello Pizzas

Prep time: 10 minutes | Cook time: 10 minutes | Serves: 2

2 large Portobello mushrooms
2 tablespoons unsalted butter, melted
½ teaspoon garlic powder
80g shredded mozzarella cheese

4 grape tomatoes, sliced
2 leaves fresh basil, chopped
1 tablespoon balsamic vinegar

1. Scoop out the inside of the mushrooms, leaving just the caps; brush each cap with butter and sprinkle them with garlic powder. 2. Fill each cap with mozzarella and sliced tomatoes. 3. Place them in the baking dish, and then bake them at 195°C for 10 minutes. 4. Garnish the dish with basil and a drizzle of vinegar, enjoy.

Per Serving: Calories 145; Fat 7.82g; Sodium 290mg; Carbs 5.81g; Fibre 1.1g; Sugar 3.75g; Protein 13.43g

Veggie Bowl

Prep time: 10 minutes | Cook time: 15 minutes | Serves: 2

90g broccoli florets
90g quartered Brussels sprouts
45g cauliflower florets
¼ medium white onion, peeled and sliced ½cm thick
½ medium green pepper, seeded and sliced ½cm

thick
1 tablespoon coconut oil
2 teaspoons chili powder
½ teaspoon garlic powder
½ teaspoon cumin

1. Combine all of the ingredients in a large bowl until vegetables are fully coated with oil and seasoning. 2. Arrange the vegetables into the air fryer basket, and then air-fry them at 180°C for 15 minutes, tossing them two or three times during cooking. 3. Serve warm.

Per Serving: Calories 111; Fat 7.66g; Sodium 106mg; Carbs 10.35g; Fibre 4.2g; Sugar 2.94g; Protein 3.6g

Chapter 3 Starter and Snack Recipes

Courgette Sticks

Prep time: 5 minutes | Cook time: 15 minutes | Serves: 4

2 small courgette
½ teaspoon garlic granules
¼ teaspoon sea salt
⅛ teaspoon freshly ground black pepper
2 teaspoons cornflour

3 tablespoons chickpea flour
1 tablespoon water
Cooking oil spray (sunflower, safflower, or refined coconut)

1. Trim the ends off the courgette and then cut into sticks about 5cm long and 1cm wide. 2. Combine the courgette sticks with the garlic, salt, pepper, cornflour, and flour in a medium bowl; add water and stir them well. 3. Spray the air fryer basket with oil and add the courgette sticks, spreading them out as much as possible. Spray the courgette with oil. 4. Air-fry the courgette at 200°C for 14 minutes until tender, nicely browned, and crisp on the outside, stirring the food and spraying them with oil halfway through. 5. Enjoy the sticks plain or with your preferred dipping sauce.

Per Serving: Calories 23; Fat 0.32g; Sodium 148mg; Carbs 4g; Fibre 0.6g; Sugar 0.47g; Protein 1.15g

Simple Courgette

Prep time: 5 minutes | Cook time: 15 minutes | Serves: 4

Cooking oil spray (sunflower, safflower, or refined coconut)
2 courgette , sliced in ½ - 1cm thick rounds

¼ teaspoon garlic granules
⅛ teaspoon sea salt
Freshly ground black pepper (optional)

1. Spray the air fryer basket with oil. 2. Place the courgette rounds in the basket and spread them out as much as you can. Sprinkle the tops evenly with the garlic, salt, and pepper (optional); spray them with oil, and roast them at 200°C for 14 minutes until the courgette rounds are nicely browned and tender, flipping the courgette and spraying them with oil halfway through. 3. Serve warm.

Per Serving: Calories 18; Fat 0.37g; Sodium 85mg; Carbs 3.12g; Fibre 1g; Sugar 2.45g; Protein 1.2g

Tamari Aubergine

Prep time: 5 minutes | Cook time: 15 minutes | Serves: 4

Cooking oil spray (sunflower, safflower, or refined coconut)	2½ tablespoons tamari or shoyu
1 medium-size aubergine (455g), cut into 1cm thick slices	2 teaspoons garlic granules
	2 teaspoons onion granules
	4 teaspoons oil (olive, sunflower, or safflower)

1. Spray the air fryer basket with oil and set aside. 2. Place the aubergine slices in a large bowl and sprinkle the tamari, garlic, onion, and oil on top. Stir them well and coat the aubergine as evenly as possible. 3. Place the aubergine in a single (or at most, double) layer in the air fryer basket. 4. Roast the aubergine slices at 200°C for 8 minutes; after 5 minutes of cooking time, transfer the aubergine slices to the bowl and toss them with the remaining liquid mixture, then place them back in the air fryer basket and resume roasting them. 5. When the cooking time is up, flip the aubergine slices and then roast them for 5 minutes longer until they are nicely browned and tender. 6. Serve warm.

Per Serving: Calories 134; Fat 4.94g; Sodium 566mg; Carbs 21.51g; Fibre 5.7g; Sugar 13.2g; Protein 3.57g

Glazed Carrots

Prep time: 5 minutes | Cook time: 20 minutes | Serves: 3

3 medium-size carrots	1 teaspoon maple syrup
1 tablespoon orange juice	½ teaspoon dried rosemary
2 teaspoons balsamic vinegar	¼ teaspoon sea salt
1 teaspoon cooking oil (sunflower, avocado, or safflower)	¼ teaspoon lemon zest

1. Trim the ends and scrub the carrots; there's no need to peel them. Cut them into spears about 2 inches long and 1cm thick. 2. Place the carrots in the baking pan, add the orange juice, balsamic vinegar, oil, maple syrup, rosemary, salt, and zest, and stir them well. 3. Roast the carrots at 200°C for 4 minutes, then stir the food and roast for 5 minutes more; when the time is up, stir them again and roast them for 5 minutes more; stir the food one last time, and resume roasting them for 4 minutes until the carrots are bright orange, nicely glazed, and fairly tender. 4. Serve warm.

Per Serving: Calories 50; Fat 1.66g; Sodium 237mg; Carbs 8.58g; Fibre 1.7g; Sugar 5.19g; Protein 0.63g

Fried Green Tomatoes

Prep time: 10 minutes | Cook time: 15 minutes | Serves: 3 to 4

120g polenta
2 tablespoons chickpea or brown rice flour
1 teaspoon seasoned salt
1 teaspoon onion granules
¼ teaspoon freshly ground black pepper

120ml nondairy milk, plain and unsweetened
Cooking oil spray (coconut, sunflower, or safflower)
2 large green (unripe) tomatoes, cut into 1cm rounds

1. Combine the polenta, flour, seasoned salt, onion, and pepper in a medium bowl; add the milk to another medium bowl. 2. Dip each tomato slice in the milk, then coat lightly with the polenta mixture, making sure to bread both sides. 3. Spray the air fryer basket with oil, place the coated slices in it in a single layer and spray the slices with oil until no dry patches of breading remain. 4. Air-fry the slices at 200°C for 6 minutes; when the time is up, spray the tops with oil again and then gently turn each tomato slice over, taking care not to overlap too much. Spray generously with oil again until no dry patches remain, and cook for another 3 minutes. 5. Spray the food with oil one last time (no need to flip them this time), and fry for another 3 to 6 minutes, or until crisp and golden-browned. 6. Finish any remaining tomatoes in batches by repeating steps 5 and 6 until you're out of tomato slices. Enjoy hot.

Per Serving: Calories 190; Fat 1.51g; Sodium 617mg; Carbs 39.63g; Fibre 3.2g; Sugar 9.85g; Protein 5.23g

Garlic Tortilla Chips

Prep time: 5 minutes | Cook time: 10 minutes | Serves: 3

4 corn tortillas
½ teaspoon garlic granules
⅛ to ¼ teaspoon sea salt

2½ teaspoons fresh lime juice
Cooking oil spray (coconut, sunflower, or safflower)

1. Cut the tortillas into quarters. 2. Place the tortillas in a bowl, and toss them with the garlic, salt to taste, and lime juice. 3. Spray the air fryer basket with the oil, add the chips, and air-fry them at 175°C for 3 minutes; tossing them and spraying them with oil halfway through. 4. Remove one last time, toss, spray with oil, and fry for 2 minutes, or until golden-browned and crisp. 5. Let the chips sit at room temperature for a few minutes before serving to finish crisping up.

Per Serving: Calories 72; Fat 0.92g; Sodium 118mg; Carbs 14.79g; Fibre 2g; Sugar 0.36g; Protein 1.87g

Low-Fat Buffalo Cauliflower

Prep time: 15 minutes | Cook time: 20 minutes | Serves: 4

For the Cauliflower
180g cauliflower florets (cut into bite-size pieces)
2 tablespoons nondairy milk, plain and unsweetened, plus 2 tablespoons
1 tablespoon ground flaxseed
50g chickpea flour
1 tablespoon cornflour

½ teaspoon garlic granules
½ teaspoon onion granules
⅛ teaspoon baking soda
Cooking oil spray (sunflower, safflower, or refined coconut)

For the Buffalo Sauce
½ teaspoon cornflour
60ml chickpea liquid, divided
60ml hot sauce

2 large garlic cloves, minced or pressed
2 teaspoons vegan margarine

For Dipping
No-Dairy Ranch Dressing, or bottled vegan ranch

1. Toss the cauliflower with 2 tablespoons of the milk and the flaxseed in a bowl, and let them rest for 5 to 10 minutes. 2. Combine the flour, cornflour, garlic, onion, and baking soda in a medium bowl. 3. Add the cauliflower to the flour mixture, and stir them well to coat the cauliflower evenly. 4. Add the remaining 2 tablespoons of milk to the small bowl and stir. Place the floured cauliflower back in the liquid and toss well. 5. Place the cauliflower back in the flour mixture. Stir them well to give the cauliflower a nice, even coating of the batter. 6. Spray the air fryer basket with oil, place the cauliflower in it and spray them with oil. 7. Air-fry the food at 200°C for 12 minutes, stirring them and spraying them with oil halfway through. 8. Combine the cornflour with a tablespoon of the chickpea liquid in a small bowl until dissolved. 9. Add the hot sauce, cornflour mixture, remaining chickpea liquid, garlic, and vegan margarine to a medium-size pot over medium-high heat, and cook them for 1 to 2 minutes until slightly thicker in texture. 10. Add the cauliflower to the buffalo sauce and toss gently to coat. Place the coated cauliflower (extra sauce and all) into a deep baking pan. 11. Air-fry the food in the air fryer for 3 minutes. Remove the baking pan, stir well, and fry another 3 to 5 minutes, until a little saucy and a little crispy. Place in a bowl, drizzle any remaining sauce on top, and serve hot with No-Dairy Ranch Dressing.

Per Serving: Calories 135; Fat 4.62g; Sodium 499mg; Carbs 18.82g; Fibre 4.3g; Sugar 5.17g; Protein 5.74g

Onion Rings

Prep time: 15 minutes | Cook time: 15 minutes | Serves: 3

½ medium-large white onion, peeled
120ml nondairy milk, plain and unsweetened
90g flour (whole-wheat pastry, chickpea, or gluten-free)
1 tablespoon cornflour
¾ teaspoon sea salt, divided

¾ teaspoon freshly ground black pepper, divided
¾ teaspoon garlic granules, divided
100g bread crumbs (whole grain or gluten-free)
Cooking oil spray (coconut, sunflower, or safflower)

1. Cut the onion into thick 1 -2 cm slices. Carefully separate the onion slices into rings. 2. Pour the milk in a small bowl. 3. To make the first breading, combine the flour, cornflour, ¼ teaspoon salt, ¼ teaspoon pepper, and ¼ teaspoon garlic in a bowl; combine the breadcrumbs with ½ teaspoon salt, ½ teaspoon garlic, and ½ teaspoon onion in another bowl to make the second breading. 4. Spray the air fryer basket with oil. 5. Dip one ring into the milk. Then, dip into the flour mixture. Next, dip into the milk again and back into the flour mixture, coating thoroughly. Dip into the milk one last time, and then dip into the breadcrumb mixture, coating thoroughly. 6. Carefully place them in the oiled air fryer basket, and spray the tops with oil; air-fry the onion rings at 200°C for 7 minutes, spraying them with oil halfway through. 7. Remove the air fryer basket and spray the onion rings with oil again. Then oh-so-gently remove and turn the pieces over, so that they cook evenly. Spray generously with oil again and fry for 4 minutes. Spray generously with oil one last time, and cook for 3 minutes, or until the onion rings are very crunchy and browned. 8. Remove them carefully and serve with ketchup or another sauce of your choice.

Per Serving: Calories 287; Fat 3.51g; Sodium 866mg; Carbs 54.74g; Fibre 5.5g; Sugar 5.48g; Protein 10.5g

Garlic Russet Potatoes

Prep time: 10 minutes | Cook time: 30 minutes | Serves: 4

455g russet baking potatoes
1 tablespoon garlic powder
1 tablespoon freshly chopped parsley

½ teaspoon salt
¼ teaspoon black pepper
1-2 tablespoons olive oil

1. Wash the potatoes and pat them dry with clean paper towels. 2. Use the fork to pierce each potato several times. 3. Season the potatoes with the garlic powder, salt, pepper and oil, and then place them in the air fryer basket. 4. Air-fry the potatoes at 180°C for 30 minutes, shaking the basket a few times throughout the cooking time. 5. Garnish the potatoes with the chopped parsley and serve with butter, sour cream or another dipping sauce if desired.

Per Serving: Calories 164; Fat 5.25g; Sodium 309mg; Carbs 26.25g; Fibre 2.9g; Sugar 1.29g; Protein 3.43g

Roasted Shishito Peppers

Prep time: 5 minutes | Cook time: 10 minutes | Serves: 3

225g shishito peppers	1 tablespoon tamari or shoyu
Cooking oil spray (sunflower, safflower, or refined coconut)	2 teaspoons fresh lime juice
	2 large garlic cloves, pressed

1. Wash the shishito peppers and set aside. 2. Spray the air fryer basket with oil, and place the peppers in it, and spritz them with oil. 3. Roast the peppers at 200°C for 6 minutes, flipping them and spraying them with oil halfway through. 4. Remove the basket one last time, shake it, and spray the peppers with oil. Roast for another 3 minutes, or until several of them have scared you with a popping sound and they've got lots of nice browned spots on them. 5. Combine the tamari, lime juice, and garlic in a medium bowl. 6. Place the shishito peppers in the bowl that contains the tamari mixture. Toss to coat the peppers evenly and serve. You'll eat the peppers with your hands and discard the stems as you go. Enjoy!

Per Serving: Calories 38; Fat 0.27g; Sodium 299mg; Carbs 8.38g; Fibre 1.2g; Sugar 3.95g; Protein 2.09g

"Samosas" with Coriander Chutney

Prep time: 20 minutes | Cook time: 10 minutes | Serves: 5

2 medium diced potatoes, cooked until tender	½ teaspoon sea salt
20g peas	½ teaspoon turmeric
2 teaspoons oil (coconut, sunflower, or safflower)	¼ teaspoon cayenne powder
3 large garlic cloves, minced or pressed	10 rice paper wrappers, square or round
1½ tablespoons fresh lime juice	Cooking oil spray (sunflower, safflower, or refined coconut)
1½ teaspoons cumin powder	
1 teaspoon onion granules	Coriander Chutney
1 teaspoon coriander powder	

1. Mash the potatoes in a large bowl, and then stir in the peas, oil, garlic, lime, cumin, onion, coriander, salt, turmeric, and cayenne until well-combined. 2. Prepare a medium bowl of water; soak a rice paper wrapper in the water for a few seconds. Lay it on a clean, flat surface. 3. Place ¼ cup of the potato filling in the centre of the wrapper and roll up any way you please. Do the same with the remaining ingredients. 4. Spray the air fryer basket with oil and place "samosas" inside, leaving a little room in between them. 5. Spray the tops with oil and air-fry them at 200°C for 9 minutes until very hot and a little crisp around the edges. 6. Let the food cool for a few minutes before enjoying with the coriander chutney.

Per Serving: Calories 205; Fat 2.46g; Sodium 331mg; Carbs 42.74g; Fibre 2.8g; Sugar 4.2g; Protein 3.6g

Kale Chips

Prep time: 10 minutes | Cook time: 10 minutes | Serves: 3

120g lightly packed kale, de-stemmed and torn into 5 cm pieces	1 tablespoon tamari or shoyu
2 tablespoons apple cider vinegar	1 tablespoon oil (olive, sunflower, or melted coconut)
1 tablespoon nutritional yeast	2 large garlic cloves, minced or pressed

1. Combine the kale pieces with apple cider vinegar, nutritional yeast, tamari, oil, and garlic in a large bowl. 2. Arrange the kale pieces into the air fryer basket and air-fry them at 160°C for 5 minutes; when the time is up, reserve any pieces that are done, and stir them and cook them for 3 minutes longer. 3. Remove any crisp, dry pieces and fry for another minute or more if needed to dry all of the kale. 4. Serve and enjoy.

Per Serving: Calories 69; Fat 4.79g; Sodium 480mg; Carbs 4.11g; Fibre 1.2g; Sugar 0.66g; Protein 2.91g

Pakoras

Prep time: 10 minutes | Cook time: 16 minutes | Serves: 5

65g chickpea flour	⅛ teaspoon cayenne powder
1 tablespoon cornflour	240g minced onion
1½ teaspoons sea salt	20g chopped coriander
2 teaspoons cumin powder	45g finely chopped cauliflower
½ teaspoon coriander powder	60ml fresh lemon juice
½ teaspoon turmeric	Cooking oil spray (coconut, sunflower, or safflower)
⅛ teaspoon baking soda	

1. Spray the air fryer basket with oil and set aside; grad a plate and set it aside as well. 2. Combine the chickpea flour, cornflour, salt, cumin, coriander, turmeric, baking soda, and cayenne in a bowl. 3. Add the onion, coriander, cauliflower, and lemon juice to the flour mixture, and stir them well, massaging the flour and spices into the vegetables. 4. Form the pakoras from the mixture, and smash them in your palm to form into a 2.5cm ball. Arrange the pakoras into the oiled air fryer basket. 5. Spray the pakoras with oil, and air-fry them at 175°C for 8 minutes, spraying them with oil halfway through cooking. 6. Remove the basket and spray the pakoras again with oil. Gently turn each one over. Spray the tops with oil and fry for 4 minutes. Remove the basket, spray generously with oil one last time, and fry for a final 4 minutes, or until very browned and crisp. 7. You can cook them in batches or store the uncooked batter in the fridge for up to 5 days. 8. Serve immediately.

Per Serving: Calories 77; Fat 1.13g; Sodium 745mg; Carbs 13.79g; Fibre 2.4g; Sugar 3.36g; Protein 3.61g

Simple French Fries

Prep time: 5 minutes | Cook time: 25 minutes | Serves: 3

2 medium potatoes, preferably Yukon Gold (but any kind will do)	½ teaspoon garlic granules
Cooking oil spray (sunflower, safflower, or refined coconut)	¼ teaspoon plus ⅛ teaspoon sea salt
	¼ teaspoon freshly ground black pepper
2 teaspoons oil (olive, sunflower, or melted coconut)	¼ teaspoon paprika
	Ketchup, hot sauce, for serving

1. Scrub the potatoes and cut them into ½ cm thick. 2. Toss the cut potato pieces with the oil, garlic, salt, pepper, and paprika in a bowl. 3. Spray the air fryer basket with oil, and place the potato pieces in it; air-fry the potato pieces at 200°C for 22 minutes until they are tender and nicely browned, stirring them every 8 minutes. 4. Serve the fries with the sauce of your choice.

Per Serving: Calories 218; Fat 3.33g; Sodium 209mg; Carbs 43.39g; Fibre 5.5g; Sugar 1.95g; Protein 5.05g

French Fries with Shallots

Prep time: 15 minutes | Cook time: 20 minutes | Serves: 3

Cooking oil spray (sunflower, safflower, or refined coconut)	¼ teaspoon sea salt
	⅛ teaspoon freshly ground black pepper
1 large potato (russet or Yukon Gold), cut into ½ cm thick slices	1 large shallot, thinly sliced
	120ml plus 2 tablespoons prepared cheesy sauce
1 teaspoon neutral-flavoured oil (sunflower, safflower, or refined coconut)	2 tablespoons minced chives or spring onions (optional)

1. Spray the air fryer basket with oil. 2. Toss the potato slices with the oil, salt, and pepper, and then place them in the oiled basket. 3. Air-fry the potato slices at 200°C for 10 minutes, stirring them after 6 minutes of cooking time. 4. Stir in the shallots and air-fry the potato slices for 9 minutes more until they are crisp and browned, stirring them once more halfway through. 5. Keep the cheesy sauce warm on a very low heat burner while cooking the potato slices. 6. Serve topped with cheesy Sauce and a sprinkle of chives or spring onions (optional).

Per Serving: Calories 123; Fat 1.69g; Sodium 507mg; Carbs 25.02g; Fibre 3.6g; Sugar 2.93g; Protein 3.25g

Berbere–Spiced Potato Fries

Prep time: 5 minutes | Cook time: 20 minutes | Serves: 2

1 large (about 340g) potato (preferably Yukon Gold, but any kind will do)	1 teaspoon coconut sugar
Cooking oil spray (sunflower, safflower, or refined coconut)	1 teaspoon garlic granules
	½ teaspoon berbere
1 tablespoon neutral-flavoured cooking oil (sunflower, safflower, or refined coconut)	½ teaspoon sea salt
	¼ teaspoon turmeric
	¼ teaspoon paprika

1. Scrub the potato and cut it into French fry shapes (about ½cm thick), in relatively uniform pieces. 2. Spray the air fryer basket with oil. 3. Toss the potato pieces with the oil, sugar, garlic, berbere, salt, turmeric, and paprika, and the place them in the oiled basket. 4. Air-fry the potato slices at 200°C for 16 minutes, flipping them halfway through. 5. When the time is up, stir them one more time and then cook them for 3 to 5 minutes more until tender and browned. 6. Serve hot.

Per Serving: Calories 214; Fat 7.34g; Sodium 593mg; Carbs 34.4g; Fibre 4.3g; Sugar 2.72g; Protein 3.9g

Glazed Brussels Sprouts

Prep time: 10 minutes | Cook time: 15 minutes | Serves: 4

Cooking oil spray (sunflower, safflower, or refined coconut)	1 teaspoon toasted sesame oil
225g trimmed Brussels sprouts	1 to 1½ teaspoons tamari or shoyu, divided
1½ tablespoons maple syrup	2 large garlic cloves, pressed or finely minced
1½ teaspoons mellow white miso	1 teaspoon grated fresh ginger
	¼ to ½ teaspoon red chili flakes

1. Spray the air fryer basket with oil. 2. Place the trimmed Brussels sprouts in the air fryer basket and spray with oil; air-fry the Brussels sprouts at 200°C for 11 minutes until they are crisp-tender and nicely browned, stirring them and spraying them with oil halfway through cooking. 3. Whisk the maple syrup and miso in a bowl until smooth; stir in the sesame oil, 1 teaspoon of tamari, garlic, ginger, and chili flakes. 4. When the Brussels sprouts are done, add them to the bowl and combine well with the sauce. Enjoy.

Per Serving: Calories 61; Fat 1.47g; Sodium 173mg; Carbs 11.26g; Fibre 2.3g; Sugar 5.92g; Protein 2.35g

Indian Okra

Prep time: 5 minutes | Cook time: 20 minutes | Serves: 4

225g okra
1 tablespoon coconut oil, melted
1 teaspoon cumin
1 teaspoon coriander
1 teaspoon garlic granules

¼ teaspoon sea salt
¼ teaspoon turmeric
⅛ teaspoon cayenne
1 teaspoon fresh lime juice

1. Toss the okras with the oil, cumin, coriander, garlic, salt, turmeric, and cayenne in a bowl. 2. Arrange the coated okras into the air fryer basket, and air-fry them at 200°C for 14 minutes until crisp, stirring them halfway through cooking. You can cook them for 6 more minutes. 3. When cooked, transfer the okras back to the seasoning bowl, sprinkle them with the lime juice and stir them well, and then enjoy.

Per Serving: Calories 52; Fat 3.64g; Sodium 150mg; Carbs 4.96g; Fibre 2g; Sugar 0.89g; Protein 1.26g

Spring Rolls

Prep time: 10 minutes | Cook time: 10 minutes | Serves: 4

4 teaspoons toasted sesame oil
6 medium garlic cloves, minced or pressed
1 tablespoon grated fresh ginger
200g shiitake mushrooms, thinly sliced
120g chopped green cabbage
120g grated carrots

½ teaspoon sea salt
16 rice paper wraps
Cooking oil spray (sunflower, safflower, or refined coconut)
Bottled Thai Sweet Chili Sauce (optional)

1. Add the toasted sesame oil, garlic, ginger, mushrooms, cabbage, carrots, and salt to a wok, and sauté them over medium heat for 3 to 4 minutes until the cabbage is lightly wilted. 2. If making with rice paper: Gently take out a piece of rice paper, run it under water, and lay it on a flat, non-absorbent surface (such as a granite countertop). Place about ¼ cup of the filling in the middle. Once the wrapper is soft enough to roll, fold the bottom up over the filling, then fold the sides in. Next, roll all the way up. Basically, make a tiny burrito. 3. Spray the air fryer basket with oil and place the spring rolls inside, leaving a little room so they don't stick to each other. 4. Spritz the top of each spring roll with oil and air-fry them at 200°C for 9 minutes until crisp and lightly browned. 5. Serve warm. You can store the leftover in refrigerate for up to 7 days.

Per Serving: Calories 278; Fat 5.45g; Sodium 511mg; Carbs 53.45g; Fibre 4.1g; Sugar 5.28g; Protein 4.86g

Fast-Cooked Courgette Rolls

Prep time: 10 minutes | Cook time: 5 minutes | Serves: 2-4

3 courgettes, sliced thinly lengthwise with a mandolin or very sharp knife
1 tablespoon olive oil

360g goat cheese
¼ teaspoon black pepper

1. Preheat your air fryer at 200°C. 2. Coat each courgette strip with a light brushing of olive oil. 3. Combine the sea salt, black pepper and goat cheese in a bowl. 4. Scoop a small, equal amount of the goat cheese onto the centre of each strip of courgette. 5. Roll up the strips and secure with a toothpick, then place them in the air fryer basket. 6. Air-fry the food for 5 minutes until the cheese is warm and the courgette slightly crispy. 7. Serve the dish with some tomato sauce on top.
Per Serving: Calories 155; Fat 13.4g; Sodium 199mg; Carbs 0.57g; Fibre 0.1g; Sugar 0.35g; Protein 8.19g

Easy-to-Cook Asparagus

Prep time: 5 minutes | Cook time: 10 minutes | Serves: 4

10 asparagus spears, woody end cut off
1 clove garlic, minced
4 tablespoon olive oil

Pepper to taste
Salt to taste

1. Preheat the air fryer at 205°C. 2. Combine the garlic and oil in a bowl. 3. Cover the asparagus with this mixture and put it in the fryer basket, and then sprinkle over some pepper and salt. 4. Air-fry the asparagus for 10 minutes. 5. Serve hot.
Per Serving: Calories 130; Fat 13.88g; Sodium 1mg; Carbs 1.66g; Fibre 0.4g; Sugar 0.75g; Protein 0.47g

Sweet Potato Chips

Prep time: 5 minutes | Cook time: 15 minutes | Serves: 2

Cooking oil spray (coconut, sunflower, or safflower)
1 small-medium sweet potato, unpeeled, thinly

sliced
¼ teaspoon dried rosemary
Dash sea salt

1. Spray the air fryer basket with oil. 2. Place the sweet potato slices in the basket, spreading them out as much as possible, and spray the tops with oil. 3. Air-fry the slices at 200°C for 12 minutes; spray them with oil and sprinkle them with rosemary and sea salt after 4 minutes; flip them and spray them with oil one more time when there are 4 minutes of cooking time left. 4. You can let them crisp up at room temperature after cooking. 5. Serve warm.
Per Serving: Calories 58; Fat 0.11g; Sodium 98mg; Carbs 13.4g; Fibre 1.9g; Sugar 4.33g; Protein 1.04g

Parmesan Courgette Chips

Prep time: 5 minutes | Cook time: 25 minutes | Serves: 2

3 medium courgette , sliced	Pepper to taste
1 teaspoon parsley, chopped	Salt to taste
3 tablespoon parmesan cheese, grated	

1. Preheat the air fryer at 220°C. 2. Put the sliced courgette on a sheet of baking paper and spritz with cooking spray. 3. Combine the cheese, pepper, parsley, and salt, and then top the sliced courgette with the cheese mixture. 4. Air-fry the food for 25 minutes until crisp. 5. Serve hot.

Per Serving: Calories 38; Fat 2.2g; Sodium 136mg; Carbs 2.33g; Fibre 0.5g; Sugar 0.02g; Protein 2.72g

Seasoned Sweet Potato Wedges

Prep time: 5 minutes | Cook time: 20 minutes | Serves: 2

2 large sweet potatoes cut into wedges	1 teaspoon cumin
1 tablespoon olive oil	1 tablespoon Mexican seasoning
1 teaspoon chili powder	Pepper to taste
1 teaspoon mustard powder	Salt to taste

1. Preheat the air fryer at 175°C. 2. Combine all of the ingredients in a bowl. 3. Transfer the coated sweet potato wedges to the air fryer basket and then air-fry them for 20 minutes, shaking the basket at 5-minute intervals. 4. Serve immediately.

Per Serving: Calories 248; Fat 7.57g; Sodium 443mg; Carbs 41.79g; Fibre 7.5g; Sugar 12.28g; Protein 4.39g

Savoury Potato Wedges

Prep time: 5 minutes | Cook time: 25 minutes | Serves: 4

4 medium potatoes cut into wedges	Pepper to taste
1 tablespoon Cajun spice	Salt to taste
1 tablespoon olive oil	

1. Place the potato wedges in the air fryer basket and pour in the olive oil. 2. Air-fry the potato wedges at 190°C for 25 minutes, shaking the basket twice throughout the cooking time. 3. Put the cooked wedges in a bowl and coat them with the Cajun spice, pepper, and salt. Serve warm.

Per Serving: Calories 319; Fat 3.93g; Sodium 23mg; Carbs 65.4g; Fibre 8.7g; Sugar 3.05g; Protein 7.7g

Chapter 4 Poultry Recipes

Lemon–Pepper Chicken Thighs

Prep time: 5 minutes | Cook time: 45 minutes | Serves: 4

For the Chicken
4 bone-in, skin-on chicken thighs (150g each)
1 teaspoon olive oil

2 teaspoons lemon pepper
¼ teaspoon salt

For the Radishes
1 bunch radishes (greens removed), halved through the stem
1 teaspoon olive oil
¼ teaspoon salt

¼ teaspoon freshly ground black pepper
1 tablespoon unsalted butter, cut into small pieces
2 tablespoons chopped fresh parsley

1. Brush both sides of the chicken thighs with olive oil, then season with lemon pepper and salt. 2. Coat the radishes, olive oil, salt, and black pepper. 3. Place the chicken skin-side up in the air fryer basket and air-fry at 200°C for 28 minutes until it reaches an internal temperature of 75°C. 4. When cooked, take out the chicken and place in the radishes; roast the radishes at 205°C for 15 minutes, scattering the butter pieces over them after 10 minutes of cooking time. 5. Stir the parsley into the radishes and serve the dish.
Per Serving: Calories 489; Fat 36.39g; Sodium 469mg; Carbs 6.29g; Fibre 1.8g; Sugar 3.28g; Protein 33.03g

Fried Turkey Wings

Prep time: 5 minutes | Cook time: 26 minutes | Serves: 4

900g turkey wings
3 tablespoons olive oil or sesame oil

3 to 4 tablespoons chicken rub

1. Put the turkey wings in a large mixing bowl. 2. Pour the olive oil into the bowl and add the rub. 3. Rub the oil mixture over the turkey wings. 4. Place the turkey wings in the air fryer basket. 5. Roast the food at 195°C for 26 minutes, flipping the wings halfway through. 6. Serve.
Per Serving: Calories 496; Fat 33.08g; Sodium 262mg; Carbs 0.6g; Fibre 0g; Sugar 0.09g; Protein 46.12g

Barbecue Chicken Drumsticks

Prep time: 10 minutes | Cook time: 35 minutes | Serves: 4

For the Drumsticks

1 tablespoon chili powder

2 teaspoons smoked paprika

¼ teaspoon salt

¼ teaspoon garlic powder

¼ teaspoon freshly ground black pepper

2 teaspoons dark brown sugar

4 chicken drumsticks

240g barbecue sauce (your favorite)

For the Kale Chips

150g kale, stems and midribs removed, if needed

½ teaspoon garlic powder

½ teaspoon salt

¼ teaspoon freshly ground black pepper

1. Combine the chili powder, smoked paprika, salt, garlic powder, black pepper, and brown sugar, and then rub the spice mixture all over the chicken. 2. Place the chicken drumsticks in the air fryer basket and bake at 200°C for 20 minutes until it reaches an internal temperature of 75°C. 3. When cooked, take out the chicken and place in the kale, sprinkling the kale with the garlic powder, salt, and black pepper; air-fry the kale at 150°C for 15 minutes. 4. Serve hot.

Per Serving: Calories 362; Fat 13.04g; Sodium 1375mg; Carbs 35.54g; Fibre 2.6g; Sugar 26.73g; Protein 25.51g

Garlic Chicken Pizza

Prep time: 10 minutes | Cook time: 40 minutes | Serves: 4

For the Pizza

2 prebaked rectangular pizza crusts or flatbreads

2 tablespoons olive oil

1 tablespoon minced garlic

180g shredded part-skim mozzarella cheese

150g boneless, skinless chicken breast, thinly sliced

¼ teaspoon red pepper flakes (optional)

For the Cauliflower "Wings"

360g cauliflower florets

1 tablespoon vegetable oil

120ml Buffalo wing sauce

1. Trim the pizza crusts to fit in the air fryer basket, if necessary. 2. Brush the top of each crust with the oil and sprinkle with the garlic. Top the crusts with the mozzarella, chicken, and red pepper flakes (if using). 3. In a large bowl, combine the cauliflower and oil and toss to coat the florets. 4. Place the pizzas in the air fryer basket and roast at 190°C for 13 minutes. 5. When cooked, take out the pizzas; add the cauliflower to the basket, and air-fry the food at 200°C for 25 minutes, adding in the Buffalo wing sauce after 20 minutes of cooking time. 6. Cut each pizza into 4 slices. Serve with the cauliflower "wings" on the side.

Per Serving: Calories 474; Fat 24.28g; Sodium 768mg; Carbs 44.2g; Fibre 4.2g; Sugar 17.8g; Protein 21.13g

Chicken Tenders with Parmesan

Prep time: 5 minutes | Cook time: 10 minutes | Serves: 4

455g chicken tenderloins	50g Italian-style bread crumbs
3 large egg whites	25g grated Parmesan cheese

1. Spray the air fryer basket with olive oil. 2. Trim off any white fat from the chicken tenders. 3. In a small bowl, beat the egg whites until frothy. 4. In a separate small mixing bowl, combine the bread crumbs and Parmesan cheese. 5. Dip the chicken tenders into the egg mixture, then into the Parmesan and bread crumbs. Shake off any excess breading. 6. Place the chicken tenders in the greased air fryer basket in a single layer. Generously spray the chicken with olive oil to avoid powdery, uncooked breading. 7. Bake the chicken tenders at 190°C for 8 minutes, flipping them halfway through. 8. Check that the chicken has reached an internal temperature of 75°C. Add cooking time if needed. 9. Once the chicken is fully cooked, plate, serve, and enjoy!

Per Serving: Calories 177; Fat 4.99g; Sodium 260mg; Carbs 3.12g; Fibre 0.1g; Sugar 0.43g; Protein 27.92g

Turkey Breast with Green Bean Casserole

Prep time: 125 minutes | Cook time: 90 minutes | Serves: 4

For the Turkey Breast

2 teaspoons unsalted butter, at room temperature	1 teaspoon poultry seasoning
1 bone-in split turkey breast (1.3kg) thawed if frozen	½ teaspoon salt
	⅓ teaspoon freshly ground black pepper

For the Green Bean Casserole

1 (260ml) can condensed cream of mushroom soup	¼ teaspoon freshly ground black pepper
120ml whole milk	455g green beans, trimmed
55g store-bought crispy fried onions, divided	30g panko bread crumbs
¼ teaspoon salt	Nonstick cooking spray

1. Spread the butter over the skin side of the turkey. Season the meat with the poultry seasoning, salt, and black pepper. 2. In a medium bowl, combine the soup, milk, ½ of crispy onions, the salt, and black pepper. 3. Place the turkey skin-side up in the air fryer basket and air-fry at 180°C for 50 minutes. 4. When cooked, take out the turkey, add the green beans to the basket, and roast the food at 175°C for 40 minutes, stirring in the soup mixture halfway through and scattering the panko and remaining 25g of crispy onions over the top and then spritzing with cooking spray. 5. Let the turkey and casserole rest for at least 15 minutes before serving.

Per Serving: Calories 469; Fat 11.49g; Sodium 1181mg; Carbs 17.18g; Fibre 3g; Sugar 7.7g; Protein 76.92g

Spicy Chicken Wings

Prep time: 10 minutes | Cook time: 25 minutes | Serves: 4

8 tablespoons unsalted butter, melted
120ml hot sauce
2 tablespoons white vinegar
2 teaspoons Worcestershire sauce

1 teaspoon garlic powder
60g plain flour
16 frozen chicken wings

1. Preheat the air fryer to 190°C. 2. In a small saucepan over low heat, combine the butter, hot sauce, vinegar, Worcestershire sauce, and garlic. Mix well and bring to a simmer. 3. Pour the flour into a medium mixing bowl. Dredge the chicken wings in the flour. 4. Place the flour-coated wings into the air fryer basket. 5. Air-fry the wings for 12 minutes, flipping them halfway through. 6. Reset the timer and fry for 12 minutes more. 7. Release the air fryer basket from the drawer. Turn out the chicken wings into a large mixing bowl, and then pour the sauce over them. 8. Serve and enjoy!

Per Serving: Calories 352; Fat 19.8g; Sodium 8954mg; Carbs 13.62g; Fibre 0.6g; Sugar 0.74g; Protein 28.3g

Turkey Meatloaf

Prep time: 15 minutes | Cook time: 50 minutes | Serves: 4

For the Meatloaf
1 large egg
60g ketchup
2 teaspoons Worcestershire sauce
50g Italian-style bread crumbs
For the Veggie Medley
2 carrots, thinly sliced
200g green beans, trimmed
180g broccoli florets
1 red pepper, sliced into strips

1 teaspoon salt
455g turkey mince (93 percent lean)
1 tablespoon vegetable oil

2 tablespoons vegetable oil
½ teaspoon salt
½ teaspoon freshly ground black pepper

1. In a large bowl, whisk the egg. Stir in the ketchup, Worcestershire sauce, bread crumbs, and salt. Let sit for 5 minutes to allow the bread crumbs to absorb some moisture. 2. Gently mix in the turkey until just incorporated. Form the mixture into a loaf. Brush with the oil. 3. In a large bowl, combine the carrots, green beans, broccoli, pepper, oil, salt, and black pepper. Mix well to coat the vegetables with the oil. 4. Place the meatloaf in the air fryer basket and roast at 175°C for 30 minutes. 5. When cooked, take out the meat; add the vegetables to the basket, and air-fry the food at 200°C for 20 minutes. 6. Serve warm.

Per Serving: Calories 702; Fat 62.32g; Sodium 1119mg; Carbs 11.33g; Fibre 2.1g; Sugar 4.94g; Protein 24.32g

Chicken Fajitas & Street Corn

Prep time: 10 minutes | Cook time: 35 minutes | Serves: 4

For the Fajitas

675g boneless, skinless chicken breasts, cut into strips

2 peppers (red, orange, yellow, or a combination), sliced into 1cm-wide strips

1 small red onion, sliced

1 tablespoon vegetable oil

2 teaspoons chili powder

1 teaspoon ground cumin

1 teaspoon salt

½ teaspoon freshly ground black pepper

½ teaspoon paprika

10g fresh coriander, chopped

Juice of 1 lime

8 (15cm) flour tortillas

For the Corn

60g mayonnaise

60g sour cream

60g crumbled feta cheese

2 tablespoons chopped fresh coriander

1 teaspoon minced garlic

½ teaspoon chili powder

4 ears corn, husked

1. In a large bowl, combine the chicken, peppers, onion, oil, chili powder, cumin, salt, black pepper, and paprika. 2. Combine the mayonnaise, sour cream, cheese, coriander, garlic, and chili powder in a shallow dish. 3. Place the fajita filling in the air fryer basket and air-fry at 200°C for 20 minutes, stirring them halfway through. 4. When cooked, take out the filling and place in the corn ears; broil the food at 230°C for 12 minutes, flipping them halfway through. 5. Mix the coriander and lime juice into the fajita filling. Divide the filling among the tortillas. Roll the corn in the mayonnaise and cheese mixture to coat. Serve hot.

Per Serving: Calories 783; Fat 28.23g; Sodium 1952mg; Carbs 105.26g; Fibre 8.1g; Sugar 19.47g; Protein 29.52g

Crispy Prawns

Prep time: 10 minutes | Cook time: 10 minutes | Serves: 8

900g prawns, peeled and deveined

4 egg whites

2 tablespoon olive oil

125g flour

½ teaspoon cayenne pepper

100g friendly bread crumbs

Salt and pepper to taste

1. Combine together the flour, pepper, and salt in a shallow bowl. 2. In a separate bowl mix the egg whites using a whisk. 3. In a third bowl, combine the bread crumbs, cayenne pepper, and salt. 4. Preheat your air fryer to 205°C on Air Fry mode. 5. Cover the prawns with the flour mixture before dipping it in the egg white and lastly rolling in the bread crumbs. 6. Put the coated prawns in the air fryer basket and top with a light drizzle of olive oil. 7. Air-fry the prawns at 205°C for 8 minutes, in multiple batches if necessary.

Per Serving: Calories 206; Fat 4.31g; Sodium 185mg; Carbs 14.8g; Fibre 0.7g; Sugar 0.71g; Protein 26.72g

Chicken with Pineapple Cauliflower Rice

Prep time: 15 minutes | Cook time: 45 minutes | Serves: 4

For the Chicken

30g cornflour , plus 2 teaspoons

¼ teaspoon salt

2 large eggs

1 tablespoon sesame oil

675g boneless, skinless chicken breasts, cut into 2.5cm pieces

Nonstick cooking spray

6 tablespoons ketchup

90ml apple cider vinegar

1½ tablespoons soy sauce

1 tablespoon sugar

For the Cauliflower Rice

175g finely diced fresh pineapple

1 red pepper, thinly sliced

1 small red onion, thinly sliced

1 tablespoon vegetable oil

180g frozen cauliflower rice, thawed

2 tablespoons soy sauce

1 teaspoon sesame oil

2 spring onions, sliced

1. Set up a breading station with two small shallow bowls. Combine 30g of cornflour and the salt in the first bowl. In the second bowl, beat the eggs with the sesame oil. 2. Dip the chicken pieces in the cornflour mixture to coat, then into the egg mixture, then back into the cornflour mixture to coat. Mist the coated pieces with cooking spray. 3. In a small bowl, whisk the ketchup, vinegar, soy sauce, sugar, and remaining 2 teaspoons of cornflour. 4. Blot the pineapple dry with a paper towel. In a large bowl, combine the pineapple, pepper, onion, and vegetable oil. 5. Place the chicken in the air fryer basket and air-fry at 205°C for 30 minutes. 6. When cooked, take out the chicken and line the basket with aluminum foil; add the pineapple mixture to the basket, and broil the food at 230°C for 12 minutes, stirring the cauliflower rice, soy sauce, and sesame oil halfway through. 7. When cooking is complete, the chicken will be golden brown and cooked through and the rice warmed through. Stir the spring onions into the rice and serve.

Per Serving: Calories 587; Fat 22.84g; Sodium 1068mg; Carbs 76.9g; Fibre 5.8g; Sugar 35.68g; Protein 20.57g

Grilled Chicken Breasts

Prep time: 5 minutes | Cook time: 15 minutes | Serves: 4

½ teaspoon garlic powder

1 teaspoon salt

½ teaspoon freshly ground black pepper

1 teaspoon dried parsley

2 tablespoons olive oil, divided

4 boneless, skinless chicken breasts

1. In a small mixing bowl, mix together the garlic powder, salt, pepper, and parsley. 2. Using 1 tablespoon of olive oil and half of the seasoning mix, rub each chicken breast with oil and seasonings. 3. Place the chicken breast in the air fryer basket. 4. Grill the chicken breast at 190°C for 14 minutes. 5. Flip the chicken and brush the remaining olive oil and spices onto the chicken halfway through the cooking. 6. Check that the chicken has reached an internal temperature of 75°C. Add cooking time if needed. 7. Once the chicken is fully cooked, transfer it to a platter and serve.

Per Serving: Calories 388; Fat 13.89g; Sodium 704mg; Carbs 0.5g; Fibre 0.1g; Sugar 0.01g; Protein 61.31g

Chicken with Roasted Snap Peas

Prep time: 15 minutes | Cook time: 45 minutes | Serves: 4

For the Chicken

40g plain flour

2 large eggs

40g cornflour , plus 2 tablespoons

675g boneless, skinless chicken breasts, cut into 2.5cm pieces

Nonstick cooking spray

2 tablespoons grated orange zest

240ml freshly squeezed orange juice

50g granulated sugar

2 tablespoons rice vinegar

2 tablespoons soy sauce

¼ teaspoon minced fresh ginger

¼ teaspoon grated garlic

For the Snap Peas

200g snap peas

1 tablespoon vegetable oil

½ teaspoon minced garlic

½ teaspoon grated fresh ginger

¼ teaspoon salt

¼ teaspoon freshly ground black pepper

4 spring onions, thinly sliced

1. Set up a breading station with three small shallow bowls. Place the flour in the first bowl. In the second bowl, beat the eggs. Place 40g of cornflour in the third bowl. 2. Bread the chicken pieces in this order: First, dip them into the flour to coat. Then, dip into the beaten egg. Finally, add them to the cornflour, coating all sides. Mist the breaded chicken with cooking spray. 3. To make the orange sauce, whisk together the orange zest, orange juice, sugar, vinegar, soy sauce, ginger, garlic, and remaining 2 tablespoons of cornflour. 4. In a large bowl, combine the snap peas, oil, garlic, ginger, salt, and black pepper. Toss to coat. 5. Place the chicken in the air fryer basket and air-fry at 205°C for 30 minutes, flipping halfway through. 6. When cooked, take out the chicken, add the snap peas to the basket, and roast the food at 190°C for 12 minutes, stirring them halfway through. 7. When cooking is complete, the chicken and vegetables will be cooked through. Stir the spring onions into the snap peas. Serve hot.

Per Serving: Calories 545; Fat 17.18g; Sodium 732mg; Carbs 75.45g; Fibre 5.2g; Sugar 25.32g; Protein 21.17g

Chicken with Broccoli

Prep time: 15 minutes | Cook time: 35 minutes | Serves: 4

For the Chicken Parmesan

2 tablespoons plain flour

2 large eggs

105g panko bread crumbs

2 tablespoons grated Parmesan cheese

2 teaspoons Italian seasoning

4 thin-sliced chicken cutlets (100g each)

2 tablespoons vegetable oil

120ml marinara sauce

60g shredded part-skim mozzarella cheese

For the Broccoli

360g broccoli florets

2 tablespoons olive oil, divided

¼ teaspoon salt

¼ teaspoon freshly ground black pepper

2 teaspoons fresh lemon juice

2 tablespoons grated Parmesan cheese

1. Set up a breading station with 3 small shallow bowls. Place the flour in the first bowl. In the second bowl, beat the eggs. Combine the panko, Parmesan, and Italian seasoning in the third bowl. 2. Bread the chicken cutlets in this order: First, dip them into the flour, coating both sides. Then, dip into the beaten egg. Finally, place in the panko mixture, coating both sides of the cutlets. Drizzle the oil over the cutlets. 3. In a large bowl, combine the broccoli, 1 tablespoon of olive oil, the salt, and black pepper. 4. Place the chicken in the air fryer basket and air-fry at 200°C for 18 minutes, flipping the chicken halfway through and spooning 2 tablespoons of marinara sauce over each chicken cutlet after 16 minutes of cooking time and topping them with the mozzarella. 5. When cooked, take out the chicken, add the broccoli to the basket, and roast the food at 200°C for 15 minutes. 6. Transfer the broccoli to a large bowl. Add the lemon juice and Parmesan and toss to coat. Serve the chicken and broccoli warm.

Per Serving: Calories 405; Fat 23.72g; Sodium 524mg; Carbs 14.72g; Fibre 2.2g; Sugar 2.79g; Protein 32.34g

Coconut Chicken Tenders

Prep time: 10 minutes | Cook time: 25 minutes | Serves: 4

For the Chicken Tenders

2 tablespoons plain flour

2 large eggs

95g unsweetened shredded coconut

80g panko bread crumbs

½ teaspoon salt

675g chicken tenders

Nonstick cooking spray

For the Utica Greens

150g frozen chopped Swiss chard, thawed and drained

15g diced prosciutto

2 tablespoons chopped pickled cherry peppers

½ teaspoon garlic powder

½ teaspoon onion powder

¼ teaspoon salt

25g Italian-style bread crumbs

25g grated Romano cheese

Nonstick cooking spray

1. Set up a breading station with three small shallow bowls. Place the flour in the first bowl. In the second bowl, beat the eggs. Combine the coconut, bread crumbs, and salt in the third bowl. 2. Bread the chicken tenders in this order: First, coat them in the flour. Then, dip into the beaten egg. Finally, coat them in the coconut breading, gently pressing the breading into the chicken to help it adhere. Mist both sides of each tender with cooking spray. 3. Place the chicken tenders in the air fryer basket in a single layer and air-fry at 200°C for 25 minutes. 4. When cooked, take out the chicken; mix the greens, prosciutto, cherry peppers, garlic powder, onion powder, and salt in the basket. Scatter the bread crumbs and Romano cheese over the top. Spritz the greens with cooking spray; and broil the food at 230°C for 10 minutes until they are soft and slightly charred. 5. Serve warm.

Per Serving: Calories 595; Fat 29.32g; Sodium 1592mg; Carbs 45.55g; Fibre 4.3g; Sugar 3.27g; Protein 38.85g

Chicken Fajitas

Prep time: 10 minutes | Cook time: 15 minutes | Serves: 4

455g chicken tenders

1 onion, sliced

1 yellow pepper , diced

1 red pepper , diced

1 orange pepper , diced

2 tablespoons olive oil

1 tablespoon fajita seasoning mix

1. Slice the chicken into thin strips. 2. In a large mixing bowl, combine the chicken, onion, and peppers. 3. Add the olive oil and fajita seasoning and mix well, so that the chicken and vegetables are thoroughly covered with oil. 4. Place the chicken and vegetable mixture into the air fryer basket in a single layer. 5. Grill the food at 175°C for 7 minutes, stirring them halfway through. 6. Reset the timer and grill for 7 minutes more, or until the chicken is cooked through and the juices run clear. 7. Once the chicken is fully cooked, transfer it to a platter and serve.

Per Serving: Calories 215; Fat 9.98g; Sodium 243mg; Carbs 6.45g; Fibre 1.1g; Sugar 1.5g; Protein 24.08g

Spicy Chicken Sandwiches

Prep time: 15 minutes | Cook time: 35 minutes | Serves: 4

For the Chicken Sandwiches

2 tablespoons flour	¼ teaspoon salt
2 large eggs	¼ teaspoon freshly ground black pepper
2 teaspoons Louisiana-style hot sauce	¼ teaspoon cayenne pepper (optional)
105g panko bread crumbs	4 thin-sliced chicken cutlets (100g each)
1 teaspoon paprika	2 teaspoons vegetable oil
½ teaspoon garlic powder	4 hamburger rolls

For the Pickles

155g dill pickle chips, drained	Nonstick cooking spray
1 large egg	120ml ranch dressing, for serving (optional)
55g panko bread crumbs	

1. Set up a breading station with three small shallow bowls. Place the flour in the first bowl. In the second bowl, whisk together the eggs and hot sauce. Combine the panko, paprika, garlic powder, salt, black pepper, and cayenne pepper (if using) in the third bowl. 2. Bread the chicken cutlets in this order: First, dip them into the flour, coating both sides. Then, dip into the egg mixture. Finally, coat them in the panko mixture, gently pressing the breading into the chicken to help it adhere. Drizzle the cutlets with the oil. 3. Pat the pickles dry with a paper towel. 4. In a small shallow bowl, whisk the egg. Add the panko to a second shallow bowl. 5. Dip the pickles in the egg, then the panko. Mist both sides of the pickles with cooking spray. 6. Place the chicken in the air fryer basket and air-fry at 200°C for 18 minutes, flipping halfway through. 7. When cooked, take out the chicken, add the pickles to the basket, and air-fry the food at 205°C for 15 minutes, shaking the basket halfway through cooking. 8. Place one chicken cutlet on each hamburger roll. Serve the "fried" pickles on the side with ranch dressing, if desired.

Per Serving: Calories 362; Fat 11.02g; Sodium 820mg; Carbs 32.71g; Fibre 2g; Sugar 4.07g; Protein 31.17g

Easy Chicken Thighs

Prep time: 5 minutes | Cook time: 20 minutes | Serves: 4

4 to 6 chicken thighs	2 tablespoons Italian seasoning
1 teaspoon salt	2 tablespoons freshly squeezed lemon juice
1 teaspoon freshly ground black pepper	1 lemon, sliced
2 tablespoons olive oil	

1. Place the chicken thighs in a medium mixing bowl and season them with the salt and pepper. 2. Add the olive oil, Italian seasoning, and lemon juice and toss until the chicken thighs are thoroughly coated with oil. 3. Add the sliced lemons. 4. Place the chicken thighs into the air fryer basket in a single layer. 5. Bake the thighs at 175°C for 10 minutes, flipping them halfway through. 6. Reset the timer and cook for 10 minutes more. 7. Check that the chicken has reached an internal temperature of 75°C. Add cooking time if needed. 8. Once the chicken is fully cooked, plate, and enjoy!

Per Serving: Calories 506; Fat 38.87g; Sodium 1046mg; Carbs 4.68g; Fibre 0.8g; Sugar 0.96g; Protein 32.2g

Chicken with Potato Salad

Prep time: 10 minutes | Cook time: 70 minutes | Serves: 4

For the "Fried" Chicken

240ml buttermilk

1 tablespoon salt

4 bone-in, skin-on chicken drumsticks and/or thighs

250g flour

1 tablespoon seasoned salt

1 tablespoon paprika

Nonstick cooking spray

For the Potato Salad

675g baby red potatoes, halved

1 tablespoon vegetable oil

120g mayonnaise

80g plain reduced-fat Greek yogurt

1 tablespoon apple cider vinegar

½ teaspoon salt

½ teaspoon freshly ground black pepper

75g shredded Cheddar cheese

4 slices cooked bacon, crumbled

3 spring onions, sliced

1. In a large bowl, combine the buttermilk and salt. Add the chicken and turn to coat. Let rest for at least 30 minutes (for the best flavour, marinate the chicken overnight in the refrigerator). 2. In a separate large bowl, combine the flour, seasoned salt, and paprika. 3. Remove the chicken from the marinade and allow any excess marinade to drip off. Discard the marinade. Dip the chicken pieces in the flour, coating them thoroughly. Mist with cooking spray. Let the chicken rest for 10 minutes. 4. In a large bowl, combine the potatoes and oil and toss to coat. 5. Place the chicken in the air fryer basket and air-fry at 200°C for 30 minutes. 6. When cooked, take out the chicken, add the potatoes to the basket, and bake the food at 205°C for 40 minutes until they are fork-tender. 7. Rinse the potatoes under cold water for about 1 minute to cool them. 8. Place the potatoes in a large bowl and stir in the mayonnaise, yogurt, vinegar, salt, and black pepper. Gently stir in the Cheddar, bacon, and spring onions. Serve warm with the "fried" chicken.

Per Serving: Calories 916; Fat 41.53g; Sodium 5152mg; Carbs 92.35g; Fibre 6g; Sugar 10.77g; Protein 42.76g

Crusted Chicken

Prep time: 15 minutes | Cook time: 25 minutes | Serves: 4

60ml buttermilk

1 large egg, beaten

200g instant potato flakes

25g grated Parmesan cheese

1 teaspoon salt

½ teaspoon freshly ground black pepper

2 whole boneless, skinless chicken breasts (about 455g each), halved

1 to 2 tablespoons oil

1. In a shallow bowl, whisk the buttermilk and egg until blended. In another shallow bowl, stir together the potato flakes, cheese, salt, and pepper. 2. One at a time, dip the chicken pieces in the buttermilk mixture and the potato flake mixture, coating thoroughly. 3. Preheat the air fryer to 205°C on Air Fry mode. Line the air fryer basket with parchment paper. 4. Place the coated chicken on the parchment and spritz with oil. 5. Cook for 15 minutes. Flip the chicken, spritz it with oil, and cook for 7 to 10 minutes more until the outside is crispy and the inside is no longer pink.

Per Serving: Calories 518; Fat 30.08g; Sodium 954mg; Carbs 7.65g; Fibre 0.5g; Sugar 1.61g; Protein 51.21g

Ranch Turkey Tenders with Vegetable Salad

Prep time: 15 minutes | Cook time: 40 minutes | Serves: 4

For the Turkey Tenders
455g turkey tenderloin
60ml ranch dressing

55g panko bread crumbs
Nonstick cooking spray

For the Vegetable Salad
1 large sweet potato, peeled and diced
1 courgette, diced
1 red pepper, diced
1 small red onion, sliced
1 tablespoon vegetable oil

¼ teaspoon salt
½ teaspoon freshly ground black pepper
60g baby spinach
120ml store-bought balsamic vinaigrette
30g chopped walnuts

1. Slice the turkey crosswise into 16 strips. Brush both sides of each strip with ranch dressing, then coat with the panko. Press the bread crumbs into the turkey to help them adhere. Mist both sides of the strips with cooking spray. 2. In a large bowl, combine the sweet potato, courgette, pepper, onion, and vegetable oil. Stir well to coat the vegetables. Season them with the salt and black pepper. 3. Place the turkey tenders in the air fryer basket and air-fry at 200°C for 20 minutes, flipping them halfway through. 4. When cooked, take out the meat, add the vegetables to the basket, and roast the food at 205°C for 20 minutes, shaking the basket halfway through. 5. Place the spinach in a large serving bowl. Mix in the roasted vegetables and balsamic vinaigrette. Sprinkle with walnuts. Serve warm with the turkey tenders.
Per Serving: Calories 744; Fat 64.19g; Sodium 383mg; Carbs 17.06g; Fibre 3.3g; Sugar 5.4g; Protein 24.92g

Maple–Mustard Glazed Turkey Tenderloin

Prep time: 10 minutes | Cook time: 55 minutes | Serves: 4

For the Turkey Tenderloin
2 tablespoons maple syrup
1 tablespoon unsalted butter, at room temperature
1 tablespoon Dijon mustard

½ teaspoon salt
½ teaspoon freshly ground black pepper
675g turkey tenderloin

For the Stuffing
150g seasoned stuffing mix
360ml chicken stock
1 apple, peeled, cored, and diced

1 tablespoon chopped fresh sage
2 teaspoons unsalted butter, cut into several pieces

1. In a small bowl, mix the maple syrup, butter, mustard, salt, and black pepper until smooth. Spread the maple mixture over the entire turkey tenderloin. 2. In the Zone 2 basket, combine the stuffing mix and chicken stock. Stir well to ensure the bread is fully moistened. Stir in the apple and sage. Scatter the butter on top. 3. Place the turkey tenderloin in the air fryer basket and air-fry at 200°C for 35 minutes. 4. When cooked, take out the meat, add the stuffing to the basket, and broil the food at 170°C for 20 minutes, shaking the basket halfway through. 5. Serve warm.
Per Serving: Calories 1167; Fat 102.24g; Sodium 827mg; Carbs 23.07g; Fibre 4.45g; Sugar 12.99g; Protein 42.03g

Southern Fried Chicken

Prep time: 15 minutes | Cook time: 26 minutes | Serves: 4

120ml buttermilk
2 teaspoons salt, plus 1 tablespoon
1 teaspoon freshly ground black pepper
455g chicken thighs and drumsticks

120g plain flour
2 teaspoons onion powder
2 teaspoons garlic powder
½ teaspoon sweet paprika

1. In a large mixing bowl, whisk together the buttermilk, 2 teaspoons of salt, and pepper. 2. Add the chicken pieces to the bowl, and let the chicken marinate for at least an hour, covered, in the refrigerator. 3. About 5 minutes before the chicken is done marinating, prepare the dredging mixture. In a large mixing bowl, combine the flour, 1 tablespoon of salt, onion powder, garlic powder, and paprika. 4. Spray the air fryer basket with olive oil. 5. Remove the chicken from the buttermilk mixture and dredge it in the flour mixture. Shake off any excess flour. 6. Place the chicken pieces into the greased air fryer basket in a single layer, leaving space between each piece. Spray the chicken generously with olive oil. 7. Air-fry the chicken pieces at 200°C for 13 minutes, flipping them and spraying them with olive oil halfway through. 8. Reset the timer and fry for 13 minutes more. 9. Check that the chicken has reached an internal temperature of 75°C. Add cooking time if needed. 10. Enjoy!

Per Serving: Calories 388; Fat 19.49g; Sodium 1316mg; Carbs 28.2g; Fibre 1.4g; Sugar 1.7g; Protein 23.46g

Crispy Butter Chicken

Prep time: 5 minutes | Cook time: 15 minutes | Serves: 2

2 (200g) boneless, skinless chicken breasts
1 sleeve Ritz crackers

4 tablespoons cold unsalted butter, cut into
1-tablespoon slices

1. Spray the air fryer basket with olive oil, or spray an air fryer–size baking sheet with olive oil or cooking spray. 2. Dip the chicken breasts in water. 3. Put the crackers in a resealable plastic bag. Using a mallet or your hands, crush the crackers. 4. Place the chicken breasts inside the bag one at a time and coat them with the cracker crumbs. 5. Place the chicken in the greased air fryer basket, or on the greased baking sheet set into the air fryer basket. 6. Put 1 to 2 dabs of butter onto each piece of chicken. 7. Air-fry the food at 190°C for 14 minutes. 8. Flip the chicken halfway through and spray the chicken generously with olive oil to avoid uncooked breading. 9. Check that the chicken has reached an internal temperature of 75°C. Add cooking time if needed. 10. Serve.

Per Serving: Calories 342; Fat 22.05g; Sodium 320mg; Carbs 24.43g; Fibre 1.8g; Sugar 6.24g; Protein 11.51g

Breaded Chicken Breasts

Prep time: 5 minutes | Cook time: 15 minutes | Serves: 2

2 large eggs
100g bread crumbs or panko bread crumbs
1 teaspoon Italian seasoning

4 to 5 tablespoons vegetable oil
2 (200g) boneless, skinless chicken breasts

1. Preheat the air fryer to 190°C on Air Fry mode. Spray the air fryer basket with olive oil or cooking spray. 2. In a small mixing bowl, beat the eggs until frothy. 3. In a separate small mixing bowl, mix together the bread crumbs, Italian seasoning, and oil. 4. Dip the chicken in the egg mixture, then in the bread crumb mixture. 5. Place the chicken directly into the greased air fryer basket, or on the greased baking sheet set into the basket. 6. Spray the chicken generously and thoroughly with olive oil to avoid powdery, uncooked breading. 7. Cook the chicken for 14 minutes, flipping and spraying it with olive oil halfway through. 8. Check that the chicken has reached an internal temperature of 75°C. Add cooking time if needed. 9. Serve.

Per Serving: Calories 538; Fat 38.75g; Sodium 501mg; Carbs 33.79g; Fibre 2.4g; Sugar 7.32g; Protein 14.82g

Chicken Parmesan

Prep time: 5 minutes | Cook time: 15 minutes | Serves: 4

2 (200g) boneless, skinless chicken breasts
2 large eggs
100g Italian-style bread crumbs

5g shredded Parmesan cheese
120ml marinara sauce
60g shredded mozzarella cheese

1. Preheat the air fryer to 180°C on Bake mode. Spray an air fryer–size baking sheet with olive oil or cooking spray. 2. Flatten the chicken breasts to about ½ cm thick. 3. In a small mixing bowl, beat the eggs until frothy. In another small bowl, mix together the bread crumbs and Parmesan cheese. 4. Dip the chicken in the egg, then in the bread crumb mixture. 5. Place the chicken on the greased baking sheet. Set the baking sheet into the air fryer basket. 6. Spray the chicken generously with olive oil to avoid powdery, uncooked breading. 7. Cook the chicken for 7 minutes. 8. Flip the chicken and pour the marinara sauce over the chicken. Sprinkle with the mozzarella cheese. Reset the timer and bake for another 7 minutes. 9. Once the chicken Parmesan is fully cooked, use tongs to remove it from the air fryer and serve.

Per Serving: Calories 212; Fat 7.99g; Sodium 426mg; Carbs 20.43g; Fibre 1.9g; Sugar 5.56g; Protein 14.09g

Chicken Drumsticks with Sweet Rub

Prep time: 5 minutes | Cook time: 20 minutes | Serves: 4

50g brown sugar	1 teaspoon dry mustard
1 tablespoon salt	1 teaspoon garlic powder
½ teaspoon freshly ground black pepper	1 teaspoon onion powder
1 teaspoon chili powder	4 to 6 chicken drumsticks
1 teaspoon smoked paprika	2 tablespoons olive oil

1. In a small mixing bowl, combine the brown sugar, salt, pepper, chili powder, paprika, mustard, garlic powder, and onion powder. 2. Wipe any moisture off the chicken. 3. Put the chicken drumsticks into a large resealable plastic bag, and then pour in the dry rub. Seal the bag. 4. Shake the bag to coat the chicken. 5. Place the drumsticks in the air fryer basket. Brush the drumsticks with olive oil. 6. Bake the drumsticks at 200°C for 10 minutes. 7. Flip the drumsticks, and brush them with olive oil. 8. Reset the timer and bake for 10 minutes more. 9. Check that the chicken has reached an internal temperature of 75°C. Add cooking time if needed. 10. Once the chicken is fully cooked, transfer it to a platter and serve.

Per Serving: Calories 331; Fat 18.94g; Sodium 1902mg; Carbs 15.58g; Fibre 0.7g; Sugar 13.52g; Protein 23.96g

Fried Turkey Breast

Prep time: 5 minutes | Cook time: 55 minutes | Serves: 4

2 tablespoons unsalted butter	1 teaspoon dried oregano
1 teaspoon salt	1 (1.5kg) boneless turkey breast
½ teaspoon freshly ground black pepper	1 tablespoon olive oil
1 teaspoon dried thyme	

1. Melt the butter in a small microwave-safe bowl on low for about 45 seconds. 2. Add the salt, pepper, thyme, and oregano to the melted butter. Let the butter cool until you can handle it without burning yourself. 3. Rub the butter mixture all over the turkey breast, and then rub on the olive oil, over the butter. 4. Place the turkey breast in the air fryer basket, skin-side down. 5. Roast the food at 175°C for 20 minutes. 6. Flip the turkey. 7. Reset the timer and roast the turkey breast for another 30 minutes. Check that it has reached an internal temperature of 75°C. Add cooking time if needed. 8. Remove the turkey from the air fryer and let rest for about 10 minutes before carving.

Per Serving: Calories 690; Fat 35.12g; Sodium 818mg; Carbs 0.41g; Fibre 0.2g; Sugar 0.01g; Protein 87.18g

Apricot Chicken

Prep time: 15 minutes | Cook time: 12 minutes | Serves: 4

210g apricot preserves
2 tablespoons freshly squeezed lemon juice
1 teaspoon soy sauce
¼ teaspoon salt

75g panko bread crumbs
2 whole boneless, skinless chicken breasts (455g each), halved
1 to 2 tablespoons oil

1. In a shallow bowl, stir together the apricot preserves, lemon juice, soy sauce, and salt. Place the bread crumbs in a second shallow bowl. 2. Roll the chicken in the pre serves mixture and then the bread crumbs, coating thoroughly. 3. Preheat the air fryer to 175°C on Bake mode. Line the air fryer basket with parchment paper. 4. Place the coated chicken on the parchment and spritz with oil. 5. Cook for 5 minutes. Flip the chicken, spritz it with oil, and cook for 5 to 7 minutes more until the internal temperature reaches 75°C and the chicken is no longer pink inside. 6. Let sit for 5 minutes before serving.

Per Serving: Calories 496; Fat 24.97g; Sodium 343mg; Carbs 17.75g; Fibre 1.8g; Sugar 12.46g; Protein 48.73g

Dill Chicken Strips

Prep time: 15 minutes | Cook time: 10 minutes | Serves: 4

2 whole boneless, skinless chicken breasts (about 455g each), halved lengthwise
240ml Italian dressing
120g finely crushed potato chips

1 tablespoon dried dill weed
1 tablespoon garlic powder
1 large egg, beaten
1 to 2 tablespoons oil

1. In a large resealable bag, combine the chicken and Italian dressing. Seal the bag and refrigerate to marinate at least 1 hour. 2. In a shallow dish, stir together the potato chips, dill, and garlic powder. Place the beaten egg in a second shallow dish. 3. Remove the chicken from the marinade. Roll the chicken pieces in the egg and the potato chip mixture, coating thoroughly. 4. Preheat the air fryer to 160°C on Air Fry mode. Line the air fryer basket with parchment paper. 5. Place the coated chicken on the parchment and spritz with oil. 6. Cook the food for 5 minutes. Flip the chicken, spritz it with oil, and cook for 5 minutes more until the outsides are crispy and the insides are no longer pink.

Per Serving: Calories 701; Fat 45.47g; Sodium 816mg; Carbs 21.24g; Fibre 0.9g; Sugar 6.57g; Protein 49.74g

Pecan-Crusted Chicken

Prep time: 15 minutes | Cook time: 15 minutes | Serves: 4

80g chopped toasted pecans
55g panko bread crumbs
1 teaspoon dried rosemary leaves, crushed
½ teaspoon salt
½ teaspoon dried sage
¼ teaspoon dried basil

⅛ teaspoon cayenne pepper
1 large egg, beaten
2 whole boneless, skinless chicken breasts (about 455g each), halved
1 to 2 tablespoons oil

1. In a blender, process the pecans for 5 to 10 seconds, or until finely ground. Add the bread crumbs, rosemary, salt, sage, basil, and cayenne. Process them for 3 seconds. Transfer to a shallow bowl. Place the beaten egg in a second shallow bowl. 2. Roll the chicken pieces in the beaten egg and the pecan mixture, coating thoroughly. 3. Preheat the air fryer to 175°C on Air Fry mode. Line the air fryer basket with parchment paper. 4. Place the coated chicken on the parchment and spritz with oil. 5. Cook for 8 minutes. Flip the chicken, spritz it with oil, and cook for 2 to 4 minutes more until the crust is flaky and the chicken is no longer pink inside.
Per Serving: Calories 579; Fat 39.12g; Sodium 473mg; Carbs 4.98g; Fibre 2g; Sugar 1.04g; Protein 50.98g

Goat Cheese–Stuffed Chicken Breast

Prep time: 10 minutes | Cook time: 35 minutes | Serves: 4

For the Stuffed Chicken Breasts
50g soft goat cheese
1 tablespoon minced fresh parsley
½ teaspoon minced garlic
4 boneless, skinless chicken breasts (150g each)
For the Courgette and Tomatoes
455g courgette , diced
150g cherry tomatoes, halved
1 tablespoon vegetable oil

1 tablespoon vegetable oil
½ teaspoon Italian seasoning
½ teaspoon salt
½ teaspoon freshly ground black pepper

½ teaspoon salt
¼ teaspoon freshly ground black pepper

1. In a small bowl, combine the goat cheese, parsley, and garlic. 2. Cut a deep slit into the fatter side of each chicken breast to create a pocket. Stuff each breast with the goat cheese mixture. 3. Brush the outside of the chicken breasts with the oil and season with the Italian seasoning, salt, and black pepper. 4. Combine the courgette, tomatoes, oil, salt and black pepper in a large bowl. 5. Place the chicken in the air fryer basket and air-fry at 200°C for 25 minutes. 6. When cooked, take out the chicken, add the vegetables to the basket, and grill the food at 230°C for 10 minutes until they are soft and slightly charred. 7. Serve hot.
Per Serving: Calories 351; Fat 14.78g; Sodium 757mg; Carbs 9.65g; Fibre 2.1g; Sugar 4.69g; Protein 44.55g

Chapter 5 Seafood Recipes

Fish Fingers

Prep time: 30 minutes | Cook time: 10 minutes | Serves: 4

375g fish, cut into fingers	1 teaspoon garlic ginger puree
100g friendly bread crumbs	½ teaspoon black pepper
2 teaspoon mixed herbs	2 teaspoon garlic powder
¼ teaspoon baking soda	½ teaspoon red chili flakes
2 eggs, beaten	½ teaspoon turmeric powder
3 teaspoon flour	2 tablespoon lemon juice
2 tablespoon Maida	½ teaspoon salt

1. Put the fish, garlic ginger puree, garlic powder, red chili flakes, turmeric powder, lemon juice, 1 teaspoon of the mixed herbs, and salt in a bowl and combine well. 2. In a separate bowl, combine the flour, Maida, and baking soda. 3. In a third bowl, pour in the beaten eggs. 4. In a fourth bowl, stir together the bread crumbs, black pepper, and another teaspoon of mixed herbs. 5. Preheat the air fryer at 175°C on Air Fry mode. 6. Coat the fish fingers in the flour. Dredge in the egg, and then roll in the breadcrumb mixture. 7. Put the fish fingers in the air fryer basket and allow to cook for 10 minutes, ensuring they crisp up nicely.

Per Serving: Calories 245; Fat 13.29g; Sodium 533mg; Carbs 8.73g; Fibre 0.8g; Sugar 1.1g; Protein 21.59g

Fish Fillet

Prep time: 10 minutes | Cook time: 5 minutes | Serves: 4

2 fish fillets, each sliced into 4 pieces	3 tablespoon polenta
1 tablespoon lemon juice	¼ teaspoon black pepper
1 teaspoon chili powder	4 tablespoon flour
4 tablespoon mayonnaise	¼ teaspoon salt

1. Preheat the air fryer at 205°C on Air Fry mode. 2. Combine together the flour, pepper, polenta, salt, and chili powder. 3. In a shallow bowl, stir together the lemon juice and mayonnaise. 4. Coat the fillets in the mayonnaise mixture, before covering with the flour mixture. 5. Put the coated fish into the air fryer basket and cook for 5 minutes, ensuring they crisp up nicely. 6. Serve hot.

Per Serving: Calories 199; Fat 10.39g; Sodium 318mg; Carbs 12.96g; Fibre 1g; Sugar 0.41g; Protein 12.69g

Lemon Fish Fillets

Prep time: 5 minutes | Cook time: 20 minutes | Serves: 2

2 teaspoon green chili sauce	2 – 3 lettuce leaves
2 teaspoon oil	4 teaspoon flour
2 egg white	2 lemons
Salt to taste	50g sugar
1 teaspoon red chili sauce	4 fish fillets

1. Slice up one of the lemons and set aside. 2. Boil a 120ml water in a saucepan. Stir in the sugar, ensuring it dissolves completely. 3. Put 125g of the flour, salt, green chili sauce, 2 teaspoons of oil and the egg white in a bowl and combine well. 4. Add 3 tablespoon of water and mix with a whisk until a smooth, thick consistency is achieved. Evenly spread the refined flour across a plate. 5. Dredge the fish fillets in the batter and cover with the refined flour. 6. Coat the air fryer's basket with a brushing of oil. Put the fish fillets in the basket and air-fry at 80°C for 10 to 15 minutes. 7. Add salt to the saucepan and combine well. Pour in the corn flour slurry and mix once more. 8. Add in the red chili sauce and stir. 9. Add the lemon slices. Squeeze the juice of the other lemon into the saucepan. Continue to cook them, ensuring the sauce thickens well, stirring all the time. 10. Take the fish out of the fryer, coat with a light brushing of oil and return to the fryer basket. 11. Allow to cook for 5 additional minutes. 12. Shred up the lettuce leaves with your hands and arrange them on a serving platter. 13. Serve the fish over the lettuce and with the lemon sauce drizzled on top.

Per Serving: Calories 511; Fat 25.96g; Sodium 393mg; Carbs 21.68g; Fibre 0.8g; Sugar 14.59g; Protein 45.91g

Cod

Prep time: 10 minutes | Cook time: 12 minutes | Serves: 5

455g cod	2 large eggs, beaten
3 tablespoon milk	½ teaspoon pepper
120g meal	¼ teaspoon salt
200g bread crumbs	

1. Combine together the milk and eggs in a bowl. 2. In a shallow dish, stir together bread crumbs, pepper, and salt. 3. Pour the meal into a second shallow dish. 4. Coat the cod sticks with the meal before dipping each one in the egg and rolling in bread crumbs. 5. Put the fish sticks in the air fryer basket. Cook at 175°C for 12 minutes, shaking the basket halfway through cooking.

Per Serving: Calories 161; Fat 3.92g; Sodium 484mg; Carbs 12.68g; Fibre 0.4g; Sugar 1.52g; Protein 17.65g

Crab Croquettes

Prep time: 10 minutes | Cook time: 20 minutes | Serves: 6

455g crab meat
100g bread crumbs
2 egg whites
½ teaspoon parsley
¼ teaspoon chives
¼ teaspoon tarragon
2 tablespoon celery, chopped

35g red pepper, chopped
1 teaspoon olive oil
½ teaspoon lime juice
4 tablespoon sour cream
4 tablespoon mayonnaise
40g onion, chopped
¼ teaspoon salt

1. Put the bread crumbs and salt in a bowl. 2. Pour the egg whites in a separate bowl. 3. Place the rest of the ingredients in a third bowl and combine thoroughly. 4. Shape equal amounts of the mixture into small balls and dredge each ball in the egg white before coating with the bread crumbs. 5. Put the croquettes in the air fryer basket and air-fry at 205°C for 18 minutes. Serve hot.

Per Serving: Calories 311; Fat 7.26g; Sodium 238mg; Carbs 33.62g; Fibre 13.7g; Sugar 0.92g; Protein 31.52g

Halibut Steak

Prep time: 55 minutes | Cook time: 15 minutes | Serves: 3

455g halibut steak
160ml low-sodium soy sauce
120ml mirin
2 tablespoon lime juice
50g sugar

¼ teaspoon crushed red pepper flakes
60ml orange juice
1 garlic clove, smashed
¼ teaspoon ginger, ground

1. Make the teriyaki glaze by mixing together all of the ingredients except for the halibut in a saucepan. 2. Bring it to a boil and lower the heat, stirring constantly until the mixture reduces by half. Remove from the heat and leave to cool. 3. Pour half of the cooled glaze into a Ziploc bag. Add in the halibut, making sure to coat it well in the sauce. Place in the refrigerator for 30 minutes. 4. Preheat the air fryer to 200°C on Air Fry mode. 5. Put the marinated halibut in the fryer and allow to cook for 10 to 12 minutes. 6. Use any the remaining glaze to lightly brush the halibut steak with. 7. Serve with white rice or shredded vegetables.

Per Serving: Calories 362; Fat 21.14g; Sodium 2172mg; Carbs 15.46g; Fibre 0.6g; Sugar 10.54g; Protein 27.21g

Broiled Tilapia Fillets

Prep time: 10 minutes | Cook time: 10 minutes | Serves: 4

455g tilapia fillets
½ teaspoon lemon pepper

Salt to taste

1. Spritz the air fryer basket with some cooking spray. 2. Put the tilapia fillets in basket and sprinkle on the lemon pepper and salt. 3. Broil the fillets at 205°C for 7 minutes. 4. Serve with a side of vegetables.

Per Serving: Calories 110; Fat 1.94g; Sodium 98mg; Carbs 0.19g; Fibre 0.1g; Sugar 0g; Protein 22.8g

Onion Salmon Patties

Prep time: 5 minutes | Cook time: 15 minutes | Serves: 4

1 egg
350g canned salmon, drained
4 tablespoon flour
4 tablespoon polenta

4 tablespoon onion, minced
½ teaspoon garlic powder
2 tablespoon mayonnaise
Salt and pepper to taste

1. Flake apart the salmon with a fork. 2. Put the flakes in a bowl and combine with the garlic powder, mayonnaise, flour, polenta, egg, onion, pepper, and salt. 3. Shape equal portions of the mixture into small patties and put each one in the air fryer basket. 4. Air-fry the salmon patties at 175°C for 15 minutes. 5. Serve hot.

Per Serving: Calories 827; Fat 14.77g; Sodium 526mg; Carbs 133.46g; Fibre 6.8g; Sugar 3.78g; Protein 35.53g

Jumbo Prawns

Prep time: 5 minutes | Cook time: 10 minutes | Serves: 4

12 jumbo prawns
½ teaspoon garlic salt
For the Sauce:
1 teaspoon Dijon mustard
4 tablespoon mayonnaise
1 teaspoon lemon zest

¼ teaspoon freshly cracked mixed peppercorns

1 teaspoon chipotle powder
½ teaspoon cumin powder

1. Sprinkle the garlic salt over the prawns and coat with the cracked peppercorns. 2. Air-fry the prawns at 200°C for 5 minutes. 3. Turn the prawns over and allow to cook for a further 2 minutes. 4. Mix together all ingredients for the sauce with a whisk. 5. Serve over the prawns.

Per Serving: Calories 125; Fat 5.32g; Sodium 232mg; Carbs 1.33g; Fibre 0.3g; Sugar 0.22g; Protein 18.17g

Cheese Tilapia Fillets

Prep time: 10 minutes | Cook time: 10 minutes | Serves: 4

455g tilapia fillets	2 teaspoon paprika
75g parmesan cheese, grated	1 tablespoon olive oil
1 tablespoon parsley, chopped	Pepper and salt to taste

1. Preheat the air fryer to 205°C on Air Fry mode. 2. In a shallow dish, combine together the paprika, grated cheese, pepper, salt and parsley. 3. Pour a light drizzle of olive oil over the tilapia fillets. Cover the fillets with the paprika and cheese mixture. 4. Lay the fillets on a sheet of aluminum foil and transfer to the air fryer basket. Fry the food for 10 minutes. 5. Serve hot.

Per Serving: Calories 226; Fat 10.7g; Sodium 399mg; Carbs 4.35g; Fibre 0.6g; Sugar 0.71g; Protein 28.52g

Salmon Croquettes with Parsley

Prep time: 5 minutes | Cook time: 10 minutes | Serves: 4

455g red salmon, drained and mashed	100g bread crumbs
80ml olive oil	½ bunch parsley, chopped
2 eggs, beaten	

1. Preheat the air fryer to 205°C on Air Fry mode. 2. In a mixing bowl, combine together the drained salmon, eggs, and parsley. 3. In a shallow dish, stir together the bread crumbs and oil to combine well. 4. Mold equal-sized amounts of the mixture into small balls and coat each one with bread crumbs. 5. Put the croquettes in the air fryer basket and air fry for 7 minutes.

Per Serving: Calories 389; Fat 28.4g; Sodium 570mg; Carbs 4.96g; Fibre 0.5g; Sugar 0.64g; Protein 27.15g

Bread-crumbed Fish

Prep time: 10 minutes | Cook time: 15 minutes | Serves: 2-4

4 tablespoon vegetable oil	1 egg
125g friendly bread crumbs	4 medium fish fillets

1. Preheat your air fryer to 175°C on Air Fry mode. 2. In a bowl, combine the bread crumbs and oil. 3. In a separate bowl, stir the egg with a whisk. Dredge each fish fillet in the egg before coating it in the crumbs mixture. Put them in air fryer basket. 4. Cook for 12 minutes and serve hot.

Per Serving: Calories 431; Fat 27.8g; Sodium 272mg; Carbs 17.77g; Fibre 1g; Sugar 2.17g; Protein 26.08g

Cream Salmon

Prep time: 10 minutes | Cook time: 10 minutes | Serves: 2

375g salmon, cut into 6 pieces	1 tablespoon dill, chopped
60g yogurt	3 tablespoon sour cream
1 tablespoon olive oil	Salt to taste

1. Sprinkle some salt on the salmon. 2. Put the salmon slices in the air fryer basket and add in a drizzle of olive oil. 3. Air-fry the salmon at 140°C for 10 minutes. 4. In the meantime, combine together the cream, dill, yogurt, and salt. 5. Plate up the salmon and pour the creamy sauce over it. Serve hot.

Per Serving: Calories 363; Fat 21.86g; Sodium 844mg; Carbs 2.74g; Fibre 0g; Sugar 1.47g; Protein 36.8g

Prawns & Bacon Slices

Prep time: 15 minutes | Cook time: 5 minutes | Serves: 4

455g prawns, peeled	455g bacon slices

1. Preheat the air fryer to 205°C on Air Fry mode. 2. Wrap the bacon slices around the prawns and put them in fryer's basket. 3. Air fry for 5 minutes and serve hot.

Per Serving: Calories 479; Fat 44.66g; Sodium 535mg; Carbs 5.06g; Fibre 0.6g; Sugar 2.84g; Protein 14.95g

Chunky Canned Fish

Prep time: 5 minutes | Cook time: 5 minutes | Serves: 4

2 cans canned fish	1 teaspoon whole-grain mustard
2 celery stalks, trimmed and finely chopped	½ teaspoon sea salt
1 egg, whisked	¼ teaspoon freshly cracked black peppercorns
100g bread crumbs	1 teaspoon paprika

1. Combine all of the ingredients in the order in which they appear. Mold the mixture into four equal-sized cakes. Leave to chill in the refrigerator for 50 minutes. 2. Put on an air fryer grill pan. Spritz all sides of each cake with cooking spray. 3. Grill at 180°C for 5 minutes. Turn the cakes over and resume cooking for an additional 3 minutes. 4. Serve with mashed potatoes if desired.

Per Serving: Calories 225; Fat 4.15g; Sodium 707mg; Carbs 5.64g; Fibre 0.6g; Sugar 0.85g; Protein 38.71g

Asian Fish

Prep time: 20 minutes | Cook time: 15 minutes | Serves: 2

1 medium sea bass, halibut or fish cutlet (275 – 300g)
1 tomato, cut into quarters
1 lime, cut thinly
1 stalk green onion, chopped
3 slices of ginger, julienned

2 garlic cloves, minced
1 chili, sliced
2 tablespoon cooking wine
1 tablespoon olive oil
Steamed rice (optional)

1. Fry the ginger and garlic in the oil until they turn golden brown. 2. Preheat the air fryer to 180°C on Air Fry mode. 3. Wash and dry the fish. Halve it, ensuring each half is small enough to fit inside the fryer. 4. Put the fish in the basket of the fryer. Pour in a drizzle of the cooking wine. 5. Place the tomato and lime slices on top of the fish slices. 6. Add the garlic ginger oil mixture on top, followed by the green onion and chili slices. 7. Top with a sheet of aluminum foil. Cook them for 15 minutes or longer if necessary. 8. Serve hot with a side of steamed rice if desired.

Per Serving: Calories 249; Fat 10.34g; Sodium 142mg; Carbs 5.7g; Fibre 0.8g; Sugar 0.85g; Protein 32.47g

Calamari Tubes

Prep time: 10 minutes | Cook time: 15 minutes | Serves: 2

240ml club soda
225g calamari tubes, about ½cm wide, rinsed and dried
170g honey
1-2 tablespoons sriracha

125g flour
Sea salt to taste
Red pepper and black pepper to taste
Red pepper flakes to taste

1. In a bowl, cover the calamari rings with club soda and mix well. Leave to sit for 10 minutes. 2. In another bowl, combine the flour, salt, red and black pepper. 3. In a third bowl mix together the honey, pepper flakes, and Sriracha to create the sauce. 4. Remove any excess liquid from the calamari and coat each one with the flour mixture. 5. Spritz the fryer basket with the cooking spray. 6. Arrange the calamari in the basket, well-spaced out and in a single layer. 7. Cook the food at 195°C for 11 minutes, shaking the basket at least two times during the cooking time. 8. Take the calamari out of the fryer, coat it with half of the sauce and return to the fryer. Cook for an additional 2 minutes. 9. Plate up the calamari and pour the rest of the sauce over it.

Per Serving: Calories 872; Fat 35.31g; Sodium 3155mg; Carbs 120.17g; Fibre 2g; Sugar 70.56g; Protein 22.82g

Crust Salmon

Prep time: 10 minutes | Cook time: 10 minutes | Serves: 5

900g salmon fillet
2 garlic cloves, minced
10g fresh parsley, chopped

50g parmesan cheese, grated
Salt and pepper to taste

1. Preheat the air fryer to 175°C on Air Fry mode. 2. Lay the salmon, skin-side-down, on a sheet of aluminum foil. Place another sheet of foil on top. 3. Transfer the salmon to the fryer and cook for 10 minutes. 4. Remove the salmon from the fryer. Take off the top layer of foil and add the minced garlic, parmesan cheese, pepper, salt and parsley on top of the fish. 5. Return the salmon to the air fryer and resume cooking for another minute.

Per Serving: Calories 326; Fat 15.84g; Sodium 969mg; Carbs 2.83g; Fibre 0.3g; Sugar 0.5g; Protein 40.62g

Parmesan Tilapia

Prep time: 10 minutes | Cook time: 5 minutes | Serves: 4

75g grated parmesan cheese
4 tilapia fillets
1 tablespoon olive oil

1 tablespoon chopped parsley
2 teaspoon paprika
Pinch garlic powder

1. Preheat your air fryer at 175°C on Air Fry mode. 2. Coat each of the tilapia fillets with a light brushing of olive oil. 3. Combine all of the other ingredients together in a bowl. 4. Cover the fillets with the parmesan mixture. 5. Line the base of a baking dish with a sheet of parchment paper and place the fillets in the dish. 6. Transfer to the air fryer and cook for 5 minutes. Serve hot.

Per Serving: Calories 224; Fat 10.72g; Sodium 400mg; Carbs 3.92g; Fibre 0.4g; Sugar 0.14g; Protein 28.81g

Cajun Prawns

Prep time: 5 minutes | Cook time: 5 minutes | Serves: 4

570g prawns, peeled and deveined
½ teaspoon old bay seasoning
¼ teaspoon cayenne pepper

1 tablespoon olive oil
½ teaspoon paprika
¼ teaspoon salt

1. Preheat the air fryer to 205°C on Air Fry mode. 2. Place all of the ingredients in a bowl and mix well to coat the prawns evenly. 3. Put the seasoned prawns in the air fryer basket and air fry for 5 minutes. 4. Serve hot.

Per Serving: Calories 173; Fat 5.37g; Sodium 1379mg; Carbs 0.29g; Fibre 0.2g; Sugar 0.04g; Protein 29.01g

Salmon Fillets

Prep time: 10 minutes | Cook time: 10 minutes | Serves: 2

2 salmon fillets
80ml of water
80ml of light soy sauce
70g sugar

2 tablespoon olive oil
Black pepper and salt to taste
Garlic powder (optional)

1. Sprinkle some salt and pepper on top of the salmon fillets. Season them with some garlic powder if desired. 2. In a medium bowl, mix together the remaining ingredients with a whisk and use this mixture to coat the salmon fillets. Leave to marinate for 2 hours. 3. Preheat the air fryer at 180°C on Air Fry mode. 4. Remove any excess liquid from the salmon fillets and transfer to the fryer. Cook for 8 minutes before serving warm.

Per Serving: Calories 692; Fat 28.6g; Sodium 1716mg; Carbs 20.94g; Fibre 0.6g; Sugar 17.5g; Protein 84.01g

Cajun Salmon

Prep time: 5 minutes | Cook time: 10 minutes | Serves: 1

1 salmon fillet
1 teaspoon Cajun seasoning
½ lemon, juiced

¼ teaspoon sugar
2 lemon wedges, for serving

1. Preheat the air fryer to 175°C on Air Fry mode. 2. Combine the lemon juice and sugar. 3. Cover the salmon with the sugar mixture. 4. Coat the salmon with the Cajun seasoning. 5. Line the base of your fryer with a sheet of parchment paper. 6. Transfer the salmon to the fryer and allow to cook for 7 minutes.

Per Serving: Calories 492; Fat 14.99g; Sodium 407mg; Carbs 3.94g; Fibre 0.5g; Sugar 1.51g; Protein 79.97g

Breaded Salmon with Cheese

Prep time: 5 minutes | Cook time: 20 minutes | Serves: 4

200g bread crumbs
4 fillets of salmon

100g Swiss cheese, shredded
2 eggs, beaten

1. Preheat your air fryer to 200°C on Air Fry mode. 2. Dredge the salmon fillets into the eggs. Add the Swiss cheese on top of each fillet. 3. Coat all sides of the fish with bread crumbs. Put in an air fryer safe dish, transfer to the fryer, and cook for 20 minutes.

Per Serving: Calories 712; Fat 29.51g; Sodium 358mg; Carbs 10.93g; Fibre 0.5g; Sugar 1.75g; Protein 94.67g

Chapter 6 Meat Recipes

T—bone Steak with Salsa

Prep time: 5 minutes | Cook time: 15 minutes | Serves: 2-3

1 (500g) T-bone steak
Salt and freshly ground black pepper
Salsa
225g cherry tomatoes
125 corn kernels (fresh, or frozen and thawed)
½ bunch sliced asparagus (2.5cm slices) (about ½

bunch)
1 tablespoon + 1 teaspoon olive oil, divided
Salt and freshly ground black pepper
1½ teaspoons red wine vinegar
3 tablespoons chopped fresh basil
1 tablespoon chopped fresh chives

1. Preheat the air fryer to 205°C. 2. Season the steak with salt and pepper and air-fry at 205°C for 10 minutes (medium-rare), 12 minutes (medium), or 15 minutes (well-done), flipping the steak once halfway through the cooking time. 3. In the meantime, toss the tomatoes, corn and asparagus in a bowl with a teaspoon or so of olive oil, salt and freshly ground black pepper. 4. When the steak has finished cooking, remove it to a cutting board, tent loosely with foil and let it rest. 5. Transfer the vegetables to the air fryer and air-fry at 205°C for 5 minutes, shaking the basket once or twice during the cooking process. 6. Transfer the cooked vegetables back into the bowl and toss with the red wine vinegar, remaining olive oil and fresh herbs. 7. To serve, slice the steak on the bias and serve with some of the salsa on top.
Per Serving: Calories 442; Fat 21.34g; Sodium 849mg; Carbs 9.57g; Fibre 2.5g; Sugar 2.8g; Protein 55.19g

Honey Mustard Ham

Prep time: 5 minutes | Cook time: 45 minutes | Serves: 6

1 (1.3kg) fully cooked boneless ham
55g packed light brown sugar
2 tablespoons honey

1 tablespoon Dijon mustard
½ tablespoon pineapple juice

1. Preheat the air fryer to 200°C. 2. Remove the ham from the package and wrap it in a large piece of aluminum foil. 3. Place the foil-wrapped ham in the air fryer basket. Air-fry the ham for 30 minutes. 4. While the ham is cooking, in a small bowl, combine the brown sugar, honey, mustard, and pineapple juice. Whisk them until well combined. 5. Remove the foil from the ham and glaze the ham all over. 6. Air-fry the food for an additional 15 minutes, reglazing every 5 minutes. 7. Slice and serve.
Per Serving: Calories 625; Fat 47.2g; Sodium 2855mg; Carbs 10.87g; Fibre 0.1g; Sugar 6.09g; Protein 37.16g

Flank Steak with Peppers

Prep time: 15 minutes | Cook time: 15 minutes | Serves: 4

60g flat-leaf parsley leaves	Freshly ground black pepper
10g fresh oregano leaves	¼ teaspoon crushed red pepper flakes
3 cloves garlic	½ teaspoon ground cumin
120ml olive oil	455g flank steak
60ml red wine vinegar	1 red pepper , cut into strips
½ teaspoon salt	1 yellow pepper , cut into strips

1. Make the chimichurri sauce by chopping the parsley, oregano and garlic in a food processor. Add the olive oil, vinegar and seasonings and process again. 2. Pour half of the sauce into a shallow dish with the flank steak and set the remaining sauce aside. 3. Pierce the flank steak with a needle-style meat tenderizer or a paring knife and marinate the steak for 2 to 24 hours in the refrigerator. 4. Remove the steak from the refrigerator and let it sit at room temperature for 30 minutes. 5. Preheat the air fryer to 205°C. 6. Cut the flank steak in half so that it fits more easily into the air fryer and transfer both pieces to the air fryer basket. Air-fry for 8 to 14 minutes, depending on how you like your steak cooked (10 minutes will give you medium for a 2.5cm thick flank steak). 7. Flip the steak over halfway through the cooking time. 8. When the flank steak is cooked to your liking, transfer it to a cutting board, loosely tent with foil and let it rest while you cook the peppers. 9. Toss the peppers in a little olive oil, salt and freshly ground black pepper and transfer them to the air fryer basket. 10. Air-fry the food at 205°C for 8 minutes, shaking the basket once or twice throughout the cooking process. 11. To serve, slice the flank steak against the grain of the meat and top with the roasted peppers. Drizzle the reserved chimichurri sauce on top, thinning the sauce with another tablespoon of olive oil if desired.
Per Serving: Calories 418; Fat 33.04g; Sodium 371mg; Carbs 4.21g; Fibre 1.3g; Sugar 1.03g; Protein 25.68g

Taco Pizza

Prep time: 10 minutes | Cook time: 10 minutes | Serves: 4

180g refried beans	4 whole-wheat pita breads
145g salsa	100g shredded pepper Jack cheese
10 frozen precooked beef meatballs, thawed and sliced	50g shredded cheddar cheese
	Cooking oil spray
1 jalapeño pepper, sliced	80g sour cream

1. In a medium bowl, stir together the refried beans, salsa, meatballs, and jalapeño. 2. Preheat the air fryer at 190°C on Bake mode. 3. Top the pitas with the refried bean mixture and sprinkle with the cheeses. 4. Once the unit is preheated, spray the crisper plate with cooking oil. Place the pizzas into the basket. 5. Bake the food for 9 minutes. 6. After about 7 minutes, check the pizzas. They are done when the cheese is melted and starts to brown. If not ready, resume cooking. 7. When the cooking is complete, top each pizza with a dollop of sour cream and serve warm.
Per Serving: Calories 503; Fat 32.52g; Sodium 695mg; Carbs 22.12g; Fibre 3.4g; Sugar 2.58g; Protein 31.54g

Steak Fajitas

Prep time: 13 minutes | Cook time: 17 minutes | Serves: 4

2 tablespoons olive oil	1 teaspoon chili powder
60ml lime juice	1 red pepper, sliced
1 clove garlic, minced	1 green pepper, sliced
½ teaspoon ground cumin	Salt and freshly ground black pepper
½ teaspoon hot sauce	8 flour tortillas
½ teaspoon salt	Shredded lettuce, crumbled Queso Fresco (or
2 tablespoons chopped fresh coriander	grated Cheddar cheese), sliced black olives, diced
455g skirt steak	tomatoes, sour cream and guacamole for serving
1 onion, sliced	

1. Combine the olive oil, lime juice, garlic, cumin, hot sauce, salt and coriander in a shallow dish. Add the skirt steak and turn it over several times to coat all sides. 2. Pierce the steak with a needle-style meat tenderizer or paring knife. 3. Marinate the steak in the refrigerator for at least 3 hours, or overnight. 4. When you are ready to cook, remove the steak from the refrigerator and let it sit at room temperature for 30 minutes. 5. Preheat the air fryer to 205°C. 6. Toss the onion slices with the chili powder and a little olive oil and transfer them to the air fryer basket. 7. Air-fry the food at 205°C for 5 minutes. Add the red and green peppers to the air fryer basket with the onions, season with salt and pepper and air-fry for 8 more minutes, until the onions and peppers are soft. 8. Transfer the vegetables to a dish and cover with aluminum foil to keep warm. 9. Place the skirt steak in the air fryer basket and pour the marinade over the top. Air-fry them at 205°C for 12 minutes. Flip the steak over and air-fry at 205°C for an additional 5 minutes. 10. Transfer the cooked steak to a cutting board and let the steak rest for a few minutes. If the peppers and onions need to be heated, return them to the air fryer for just 1 to 2 minutes. 11. Thinly slice the steak at an angle, cutting against the grain of the steak. 12. Serve the steak with the onions and peppers, the warm tortillas and the fajita toppings on the side so that everyone can make their own fajita.
Per Serving: Calories 582; Fat 24.02g; Sodium 1458mg; Carbs 52.38g; Fibre 3.1g; Sugar 4.73g; Protein 39.74g

Pork Chops

Prep time: 10 minutes | Cook time: 15 minutes | Serves: 4

1 teaspoon garlic powder	Salt
1 teaspoon dried garlic flakes	Freshly ground black pepper
1 teaspoon dried parsley	4 (1cm thick) boneless pork chops
½ teaspoon dried rosemary	1 tablespoon extra-virgin olive oil, plus more for
½ teaspoon dried thyme	spraying

1. Preheat the air fryer to 190°C. 2. In a small bowl, combine the garlic powder, garlic flakes, parsley, rosemary, thyme, salt, and pepper. 3. Rub both sides of the pork chops with the olive oil, and then coat each side with the garlic-herb mixture. 4. Lightly spray the air fryer basket with oil. Place the coated pork chops in a single layer in the basket, leaving ½ cm between each to ensure even cooking. 5. Air fry for 4 to 5 minutes. Flip the pork chops and cook for an additional 4 to 5 minutes, or until they reach an internal temperature of at least 60°C. 6. Let the pork chops rest for 5 minutes before cutting. Serve warm.
Per Serving: Calories 269; Fat 9.75g; Sodium 130mg; Carbs 0.88g; Fibre 0.1g; Sugar 0.03g; Protein 41.65g

Balsamic Marinated Rib Eye Steak

Prep time: 15 minutes | Cook time: 16 minutes | Serves: 2

3 tablespoons balsamic vinegar	Coarsely ground black pepper
2 cloves garlic, sliced	Salt
1 tablespoon Dijon mustard	1 (200g) bag cipollini onions, peeled
1 teaspoon fresh thyme leaves	1 teaspoon balsamic vinegar
1 (400g) boneless rib eye steak	

1. Combine the 3 tablespoons of balsamic vinegar, garlic, Dijon mustard and thyme in a small bowl. Pour this marinade over the steak. 2. Pierce the steak several times with a paring knife ora needle-style meat tenderizer and season it generously with coarsely ground black pepper. 3. Flip the steak over and pierce the other side in a similar fashion, seasoning again with the coarsely ground black pepper. 4. Marinate the steak for 2 to 24 hours in the refrigerator. When you are ready to cook, remove the steak from the refrigerator and let it sit at room temperature for 30 minutes. 5. Preheat the air fryer to 205°C. 6. Season the steak with salt and air-fry at 205°C for 12 minutes (medium-rare), 14 minutes (medium), or 16 minutes (well-done), flipping the steak once half way through the cooking time. 7. While the steak is air-frying, toss the onions with 1 teaspoon of balsamic vinegar and season with salt. 8. Remove the steak from the air fryer and let it rest while you fry the onions. 9. Transfer the onions to the air fryer basket and air-fry for 10 minutes, adding a few more minutes if your onions are very large. Then, slice the steak on the bias and serve with the fried onions on top.
Per Serving: Calories 342; Fat 13.84g; Sodium 272mg; Carbs 18.58g; Fibre 1.9g; Sugar 12.39g; Protein 35.83g

Spicy Grilled Steak

Prep time: 25 minutes | Cook time: 18 minutes | Serves: 4

2 tablespoons salsa	⅛ teaspoon red pepper flakes
1 tablespoon minced chipotle pepper	150g sirloin tip steak, cut into 4 pieces and gently
1 tablespoon apple cider vinegar	pounded to about 1 cm thick
1 teaspoon ground cumin	Cooking oil spray
⅛ teaspoon freshly ground black pepper	

1. In a small bowl, thoroughly mix the salsa, chipotle pepper, vinegar, cumin, black pepper, and red pepper flakes. Rub this mixture into both sides of each steak piece. Let stand for 15 minutes at room temperature. 2. Preheat the air fryer at 200°C on Air Fry mode. 3. Once the unit is preheated, spray the crisper plate with cooking oil. 4. Cook the food for 9 minutes. 5. After about 6 minutes, check the steaks. If a food thermometer inserted into the meat registers at least 60°C, they are done. If not, resume cooking. 6. When the cooking is done, transfer the steaks to a clean plate and cover with aluminum foil to keep warm. 7. Thinly slice the steaks against the grain and serve.
Per Serving: Calories 107; Fat 4.99g; Sodium 291mg; Carbs 8.13g; Fibre 1.4g; Sugar 2.22g; Protein 7.51g

Beef Spinach Braciole

Prep time: 20 minutes | Cook time: 60 minutes | Serves: 4

½ onion, finely chopped
1 teaspoon olive oil
80ml red wine
300g crushed tomatoes
1 teaspoon Italian seasoning
½ teaspoon garlic powder
¼ teaspoon crushed red pepper flakes
2 tablespoons chopped fresh parsley

2 top round steaks (about 675g)
Salt and freshly ground black pepper
60g fresh spinach, chopped
1 clove minced garlic
75g roasted red peppers, julienned
50g grated pecorino cheese
35g pine nuts, toasted and rough chopped
2 tablespoons olive oil

1. Preheat the air fryer to 205°C. 2. Toss the onions and olive oil together in a 18 cm metal baking pan or casserole dish. 3. Air-fry the food at 205°C for 5 minutes, stirring a couple times during the cooking process. Add the red wine, crushed tomatoes, Italian seasoning, garlic powder, red pepper flakes and parsley and stir. 4. Cover the pan tightly with aluminum foil, lower the air fryer temperature to 175°C and continue to air-fry for 15 minutes. 5. While the sauce is simmering, prepare the beef. Using a meat mallet, pound the beef until it is ½ cm thick. Season both sides of the beef with salt and pepper. Combine the spinach, garlic, red peppers, pecorino cheese, pine nuts and olive oil in a medium bowl. 6. Season them with salt and freshly ground black pepper. Spread the mixture evenly over the steaks. 7. Starting at one of the short ends, roll the beef around the filling, tucking in the sides as you roll to ensure the filling is completely enclosed. Secure the beef rolls with toothpicks. 8. Remove the baking pan with the sauce from the air fryer and set it aside. 9. Preheat the air fryer to 205°C. 10. Brush or spray the beef rolls with a little olive oil and air-fry at 205°C for 12 minutes, rotating the beef during the cooking process for even browning. 11. When the beef is browned, submerge the rolls into the sauce in the baking pan, cover the pan with foil and return it to the air fryer. 12. Air-fry at 120°C for 60 minutes. 13. Remove the beef rolls from the sauce. Cut each roll into slices and serve with pasta, ladling some of the sauce over top.

Per Serving: Calories 434; Fat 22.59g; Sodium 400mg; Carbs 10.12g; Fibre 2.2g; Sugar 3.91g; Protein 46.32g

Rib Eye Cheesesteaks

Prep time: 15 minutes | Cook time: 20 minutes | Serves: 2

1 (300g) rib eye steak
2 tablespoons Worcestershire sauce
Salt and freshly ground black pepper
½ onion, sliced

2 tablespoons butter, melted
100g sliced Cheddar or provolone cheese
2 long hoagie rolls, lightly toasted

1. Place the steak in the freezer for 30 minutes to make it easier to slice. When it is well-chilled, thinly slice the steak against the grain and transfer it to a bowl. 2. Pour the Worcestershire sauce over the steak and season it with salt and pepper. Allow the meat to come to room temperature. 3. Preheat the air fryer to 205°C. 4. Toss the sliced onion with the butter and transfer it to the air fryer basket. 5. Air-fry the food at 205°C for 12 minutes, shaking the basket a few times during the cooking process. 6. Place the steak on top of the onions and air-fry for another 6 minutes, stirring the meat and onions together halfway through the cooking time. 7. When the air fryer has finished cooking, divide the steak and onions in half in the air fryer basket, pushing each half to one side of the air fryer basket. 8. Place the cheese on top of each half, push the drawer back into the turned off air fryer and let it sit for 2 minutes, until the cheese has melted. 9. Transfer each half of the cheesesteak mixture into a toasted roll with the cheese side up and dig in!

Per Serving: Calories 800; Fat 64.26g; Sodium 988mg; Carbs 5.38g; Fibre 0.1g; Sugar 2.13g; Protein 50.31g

Roast Beef with Potatoes

Prep time: 15 minutes | Cook time: 60 minutes | Serves: 8-10

1 (2.3kg) top sirloin roast
Salt and freshly ground black pepper
1 teaspoon dried thyme
900g red potatoes, halved or quartered

2 teaspoons olive oil
1 teaspoon very finely chopped fresh rosemary, plus more for garnish

1. Preheat the air fryer to 180°C. 2. Season the beef all over with salt, pepper and thyme. Transfer the seasoned roast to the air fryer basket. 3. Air-fry the beef at 180°C for 20 minutes. 4. Turn the roast over and continue to air-fry at 180°C for another 20 minutes. 5. Toss the potatoes with the olive oil, salt, pepper and fresh rosemary. Turn the roast over again in the air fryer basket and toss the potatoes in around the sides of the roast. 6. Air-fry the roast and potatoes at 180°C for another 20 minutes. (Rare – 55°C, Medium – 65°C, Well done – 75°C). Let the roast rest for 5 to 10 minutes before slicing and serving. 7. While the roast is resting, continue to air-fry the potatoes if desired for extra browning and crispiness. 8. Slice the roast and serve with the potatoes, adding a little more fresh rosemary if desired.

Per Serving: Calories 217; Fat 9.22g; Sodium 75mg; Carbs 15.24g; Fibre 1.6g; Sugar 1.17g; Protein 18.86g

Cranberry Burgers

Prep time: 15 minutes | Cook time: 10 minutes | Serves: 4

455g beef mince (80% lean)	1 (100g) wheel of Brie cheese, sliced
1 tablespoon chopped fresh thyme	Handful of rocket
1 tablespoon Worcestershire sauce	3 or 4 brioche hamburger buns (or potato
½ teaspoon salt	hamburger buns), toasted
Freshly ground black pepper	60 – 120g whole berry cranberry sauce

1. Combine the beef, thyme, Worcestershire sauce, salt and pepper together in a large bowl and mix well. Divide the meat into 4 (115g) portions or 3 larger portions and then form them into burger patties, being careful not to over-handle the meat. 2. Preheat the air fryer to 200°C and pour a little water into the bottom of the air fryer drawer. (This will help prevent the grease that drips into the bottom drawer from burning and smoking.). 3. Transfer the burgers to the air fryer basket. Air-fry the burgers at 200°C for 5 minutes. Flip the burgers over and air-fry for another 2 minutes. Top each burger with a couple slices of brie and air-fry for another minute or two, just to soften the cheese. 4. Build the burgers by placing a few leaves of rocket on the bottom bun, adding the burger and a spoonful of cranberry sauce on top. 5. Top with the other half of the hamburger bun and enjoy.

Per Serving: Calories 627; Fat 32.2g; Sodium 1012mg; Carbs 34.54g; Fibre 2g; Sugar 12.7g; Protein 48.98g

Beef & Broccoli

Prep time: 10 minutes | Cook time: 18 minutes | Serves: 4

2 tablespoons cornflour	1 onion, chopped
120ml low-sodium beef stock	100g sliced cremini mushrooms
1 teaspoon low-sodium soy sauce	1 tablespoon grated peeled fresh ginger
150g sirloin strip steak, cut into 2.5cm cubes	Cooked brown rice (optional), for serving
225g broccoli florets	

1. In a medium bowl, stir together the cornflour, beef stock, and soy sauce until the cornflour is completely dissolved. 2. Add the beef cubes and toss to coat. Let stand for 5 minutes at room temperature. 3. Preheat the air fryer at 205°C on Air Fry mode. 4. Once the unit is preheated, use a slotted spoon to transfer the beef from the stock mixture into a medium metal bowl that fits into the basket. Reserve the stock. 5. Add the broccoli, onion, mushrooms, and ginger to the beef. Place the bowl into the basket. 6. Cook the food for 18 minutes. 7. After about 12 minutes, check the beef and broccoli. 8. When the cooking is complete, serve immediately over hot cooked brown rice, if desired.

Per Serving: Calories 155; Fat 3.18g; Sodium 105mg; Carbs 10.32g; Fibre 1.3g; Sugar 1.59g; Protein 22.25g

Beef Lettuce Wraps

Prep time: 15 minutes | Cook time: 15 minutes | Serves: 4

80ml low-sodium soy sauce

2 teaspoons fish sauce

2 teaspoons brown sugar

1 tablespoon chili paste

Juice of 1 lime

2 cloves garlic, minced

2 teaspoons fresh ginger, minced

Serving

1 head butter lettuce

60g julienned carrots

60g julienned cucumber

455g beef sirloin

Sauce

80ml low-sodium soy sauce

Juice of 2 limes

1 tablespoon mirin wine

2 teaspoons chili paste

60g sliced radishes, sliced into half moons

350g cooked rice noodles

50g chopped peanuts

1. Combine the soy sauce, fish sauce, brown sugar, chili paste, lime juice, garlic and ginger in a bowl. Slice the beef into thin slices, and then cut those slices in half. 2. Add the beef to the marinade and marinate for 1 to 3 hours in the refrigerator. 3. When you are ready to cook, remove the steak from the refrigerator and let it sit at room temperature for 30 minutes. 4. Preheat the air fryer to 205°C. 5. Transfer the beef and marinade to the air fryer basket. Air-fry them at 205°C for 12 minutes, shaking the basket a few times during the cooking process. 6. While the beef is cooking, prepare a wrap-building station. Combine the soy sauce, lime juice, mirin wine and chili paste in a bowl and transfer to a little pouring vessel. Separate the lettuce leaves from the head of lettuce and put them in a serving bowl. Place the carrots, cucumber, radish, rice noodles and chopped peanuts all in separate serving bowls. 7. When the beef has finished cooking, transfer it to another serving bowl and invite your guests to build their wraps. 8. Place some beef in a lettuce leaf and top with carrots, cucumbers, some rice noodles and chopped peanuts. Drizzle a little sauce over top, fold the lettuce around the ingredients and enjoy!

Per Serving: Calories 491; Fat 21.57g; Sodium 2063mg; Carbs 40.11g; Fibre 4.3g; Sugar 5.5g; Protein 36.08g

Beef Cheese Empanadas

Prep time: 15 minutes | Cook time: 25 minutes | Serves: 5

Cooking oil spray	Salt
2 garlic cloves, chopped	Freshly ground black pepper
50g chopped green pepper	15 empanada wrappers
⅓ medium onion, chopped	120g shredded mozzarella cheese
200g 93% lean beef mince	100g shredded pepper Jack cheese
1 teaspoon hamburger seasoning	1 tablespoon butter

1. Spray a frying pan with the cooking oil and place it over medium-high heat. Add the garlic, green pepper, and onion. Cook them for 2 minutes until fragrant. 2. Add the beef mince to the frying pan. Season it with the hamburger seasoning, salt, and pepper. 3. Break up the beef into small pieces. Cook the beef for about 5 minutes until browned. Drain any excess fat. 4. Lay the empanada wrappers on a work surface. 5. Dip a basting brush in water. Glaze each wrapper along the edges with the wet brush. 6. Scoop 2 to 3 tablespoons of the beef mince mixture onto each empanada wrapper. Sprinkle the mozzarella and pepper Jack cheeses over the beef. 7. Close the empanadas by folding the empanada wrapper in half over the filling. Press along the edges to seal. 8. Preheat the air fryer at 205°C on Air Fry mode. 9. Once the unit is preheated, spray the crisper plate with cooking oil. Arrange the food into the basket and spray each with cooking oil. 10. Cook them for 10 minutes. 11. After 8 minutes, flip the empanadas and spray them with more cooking oil. Resume cooking. 12. When the cooking is complete, transfer the empanadas to a plate. For added flavour, top each hot empanada with a bit of butter and let melt. 13. Cool for 5 minutes before serving.

Per Serving: Calories 523; Fat 15.85g; Sodium 973mg; Carbs 58.45g; Fibre 2.4g; Sugar 0.99g; Protein 34.37g

Meatballs in Tomato Sauce

Prep time: 10 minutes | Cook time: 15 minutes | Serves: 4

3 spring onions, minced	Freshly ground black pepper
1 garlic clove, minced	455g 95% lean beef mince
1 egg yolk	Olive oil spray
35g cracker crumbs	300ml any tomato pasta sauce
Pinch salt	2 tablespoons Dijon mustard

1. In a large bowl, combine the spring onions, garlic, egg yolk, cracker crumbs, salt, and pepper and mix well. 2. Add the beef mince and gently but thoroughly mix with your hands until combined. Form the meat mixture into 1 cm round meatballs. 3. Preheat the air fryer at 205°C on Bake mode. 4. Once the unit is preheated, spray the crisper plate with olive oil. Working in batches, spray the meatballs with olive oil and place them into the basket in a single layer, without touching. 5. Cook the meatballs for 11 minutes. 6. When the cooking is complete, a food thermometer inserted into the meatballs should register 75°C. Transfer the meatballs to a 15 cm metal bowl. 7. Top the meatballs with the pasta sauce and Dijon mustard, and mix gently. Place the bowl into the basket. 8. Cook the food for 4 minutes. 9. When the cooking is complete, serve hot.

Per Serving: Calories 319; Fat 14.34g; Sodium 402mg; Carbs 12.39g; Fibre 1.3g; Sugar 3.34g; Protein 33.07g

Panko Boneless Pork Chops

Prep time: 10 minutes | Cook time: 15 minutes | Serves: 4

4 centre-cut boneless pork chops, excess fat trimmed	1½ teaspoons paprika
¼ teaspoon salt	½ teaspoon granulated garlic
2 eggs	½ teaspoon onion powder
165g panko bread crumbs	1 teaspoon chili powder
3 tablespoons grated Parmesan cheese	¼ teaspoon freshly ground black pepper
	Olive oil spray

1. Sprinkle the pork chops with salt on both sides and let them sit while you prepare the seasonings and egg wash. 2. In a shallow medium bowl, beat the eggs. 3. In another shallow medium bowl, stir together the panko, Parmesan cheese, paprika, granulated garlic, onion powder, chili powder, and pepper. 4. Dip the pork chops in the egg and in the panko mixture to coat. Firmly press the crumbs onto the chops. 5. Preheat the air fryer at 205°C on Roast mode. 6. Once the unit is preheated, spray the crisper plate with olive oil. Place the pork chops into the basket and spray them with olive oil. 7. Roast the food for 12 minutes. 8. After 6 minutes, flip the pork chops and spray them with more olive oil. Resume cooking. 9. When the cooking is complete, the chops should be golden and crispy and a food thermometer should register 60°C. 10. Serve immediately.

Per Serving: Calories 348; Fat 13.12g; Sodium 452mg; Carbs 8.77g; Fibre 1g; Sugar 1.24g; Protein 46.14g

Lemon Pork Tenderloin

Prep time: 5 minutes | Cook time: 10 minutes | Serves: 4

1 (455g) pork tenderloin, cut into 1cm-thick slices	½ teaspoon dried marjoram leaves
1 tablespoon extra-virgin olive oil	Pinch salt
1 tablespoon freshly squeezed lemon juice	Freshly ground black pepper
1 tablespoon honey	Cooking oil spray
½ teaspoon grated lemon zest	

1. Put the pork slices in a medium bowl. 2. In a small bowl, whisk the olive oil, lemon juice, honey, lemon zest, marjoram, salt, and pepper until combined. Pour this marinade over the tenderloin slices and gently massage with your hands to work it into the pork. 3. Preheat the air fryer at 205°C on Roast mode. 4. Once the unit is preheated, spray the crisper plate with cooking oil. Place the pork into the basket. 5. Roast the food for 10 minutes. 6. When the cooking is complete, a food thermometer inserted into the pork should register at least 60°C. Let the pork stand for 5 minutes and serve.

Per Serving: Calories 150; Fat 4.44g; Sodium 117mg; Carbs 4.69g; Fibre 0.1g; Sugar 4.43g; Protein 21.84g

Barbecued Back Ribs

Prep time: 30 minutes | Cook time: 30 minutes | Serves: 4

1 (2.7kg) rack baby back ribs	Salt
1 teaspoon onion powder	Freshly ground black pepper
1 teaspoon garlic powder	Cooking oil spray
1 teaspoon light brown sugar	120ml barbecue sauce
1 teaspoon dried oregano	

1. Remove the thin membrane from the back of the ribs. Cut the rack in half, or as needed, so the ribs fit in the air fryer basket. The best way to do this is to cut the ribs into 4 or 5-rib sections. 2. In a small bowl, stir together the onion powder, garlic powder, brown sugar, and oregano and season with salt and pepper. Rub the spice seasoning onto the front and back of the ribs. 3. Cover the ribs with plastic wrap or foil and let sit at room temperature for 30 minutes. 4. Preheat the air fryer at 205°C on Roast mode. 5. Once the unit is preheated, spray the crisper plate with cooking oil. Place the ribs into the basket. 6. Roast the food for 30 minutes. 7. After 15 minutes, flip the ribs. Resume cooking for 15 minutes until a food thermometer registers 90°C. 8. When the cooking is complete, transfer the ribs to a serving dish. Drizzle the ribs with the barbecue sauce and serve.

Per Serving: Calories 934; Fat 61.67g; Sodium 638mg; Carbs 17.71g; Fibre 0.6g; Sugar 13.07g; Protein 77.48g

Pork Teriyaki

Prep time: 10 minutes | Cook time: 15 minutes | Serves: 4

1 head broccoli, trimmed into florets
1 tablespoon extra-virgin olive oil
¼ teaspoon sea salt
¼ teaspoon freshly ground black pepper
455g pork tenderloin, trimmed and cut into 2.5cm pieces
120ml teriyaki sauce, divided
Olive oil spray
400g cooked brown rice
Sesame seeds, for garnish

1. Preheat the air fryer at 205°C on Roast mode. 2. In a large bowl, toss together the broccoli, olive oil, salt, and pepper. 3. In a medium bowl, toss together the pork and 3 tablespoons of teriyaki sauce to coat the meat. 4. Once the unit is preheated, spray the crisper plate with olive oil. Put the broccoli and pork into the basket. Spray them with olive oil and drizzle with 1 tablespoon of teriyaki sauce. 5. Roast the food for 13 minutes. 6. After 10 to 12 minutes, the broccoli is tender and light golden brown and a food thermometer inserted into the pork should register 60°C. Remove the basket and drizzle the broccoli and pork with the remaining teriyaki sauce and toss to coat. Reinsert the basket to resume cooking for 1 minute. 7. When the cooking is complete, serve immediately over the hot cooked rice, if desired, garnished with the sesame seeds.

Per Serving: Calories 317; Fat 6.39g; Sodium 887mg; Carbs 28.23g; Fibre 2g; Sugar 5.44g; Protein 34.51g

Greek Lamb Burgers

Prep time: 10 minutes | Cook time: 18 minutes | Serves: 4

1 teaspoon ground ginger
½ teaspoon ground coriander
¼ teaspoon freshly ground white pepper
½ teaspoon ground cinnamon
½ teaspoon dried oregano
¼ teaspoon ground allspice
¼ teaspoon ground turmeric
120g low-fat plain Greek yogurt
455g lamb mince
1 teaspoon garlic paste
¼ teaspoon salt
¼ teaspoon freshly ground black pepper
Cooking oil spray
4 hamburger buns
½ cucumber, thinly sliced

1. In a small bowl, stir together the ginger, coriander, white pepper, cinnamon, oregano, allspice, and turmeric. 2. Put the yogurt in a small bowl and add half the spice mixture. Mix well and refrigerate them until ready to use. 3. Preheat the air fryer at 180°C on Air Fry mode. 4. In a large bowl, combine the lamb, garlic paste, remaining spice mix, salt, and pepper. Gently but thoroughly mix the ingredients with your hands. Form the meat into 4 patties. 5. Once the unit is preheated, spray the crisper plate with cooking oil, and place the patties into the basket. 6. Cook the patties for 18 minutes. 7. After 15 minutes, check the burgers. If a food thermometer inserted into the burgers registers 160°C, the burgers are done. If not, resume cooking. 8. When the cooking is complete, assemble the burgers on the buns with cucumber slices and a dollop of the yogurt dip.

Per Serving: Calories 297; Fat 15.27g; Sodium 330mg; Carbs 13.39g; Fibre 1g; Sugar 3.34g; Protein 26.61g

Chicken Steak

Prep time: 15 minutes | Cook time: 10 minutes | Serves: 4

4 beef cube steaks
Salt
Freshly ground black pepper
125g plain flour
½ teaspoon garlic powder
½ teaspoon onion powder

½ teaspoon smoked paprika
¼ teaspoon cayenne pepper
1 large egg
120ml buttermilk
Extra-virgin olive oil, for the basket

1. Preheat the air fryer to 205°C on Air Fry mode. 2. Season the beef generously with salt and black pepper. 3. In a small shallow bowl, mix together the flour, garlic powder, onion powder, smoked paprika, cayenne pepper, and a pinch of salt. 4. In a second small shallow bowl, combine the egg, buttermilk, and a pinch of salt. Whisk until smooth. 5. Coat each beef cube steak in the flour mixture, then in the buttermilk mixture, then in the flour mixture again. 6. Lightly spray the air fryer basket with oil. Place the coated cube steaks in a single layer in the basket, leaving ½ cm between each to ensure even cooking. 7. Air fry them for 4 to 5 minutes. Flip the steaks and air fry for an additional 4 to 5 minutes, or until they have reached an internal temperature of 60°C.
Per Serving: Calories 470; Fat 14.61g; Sodium 235mg; Carbs 26.24g; Fibre 1.1g; Sugar 1.65g; Protein 54.31g

Jerk–Flavoured Pork Loin

Prep time: 10 minutes | Cook time: 20 minutes | Serves: 4

2 tablespoons extra-virgin olive oil, plus more for the basket
2 tablespoons light brown sugar
2 teaspoons allspice
1 teaspoon salt
½ teaspoon ground cumin

½ teaspoon freshly ground black pepper
½ teaspoon cayenne pepper
½ teaspoon red pepper flakes
¼ teaspoon ground cloves
¼ teaspoon ground cinnamon
675g pork loin roast, trimmed of fat

1. Preheat the air fryer to 200°C. 2. In a small bowl, combine the extra-virgin olive oil, brown sugar, allspice, salt, cumin, black pepper, cayenne pepper, red pepper flakes, cloves, and cinnamon. Stir to create a thick paste. 3. Cut the pork loin roast into large pieces that are no thicker than 1cm. 4. Rub the jerk seasoning paste into the pork pieces, coating on all sides. Transfer the coated pork to a container. Cover and refrigerate for at least 4 hours and up to overnight. 5. Let the pork sit on the counter for 20 minutes to come to room temperature. 6. Lightly spray the air fryer basket with oil. Place the pork in a single layer in the basket, leaving ½ cm between each piece to ensure even cooking. 7. Air fry for 10 minutes. Flip the pork and air fry for an additional 10 minutes, or until it has reached an internal temperature of at least 60°C.
Per Serving: Calories 403; Fat 22.01g; Sodium 662mg; Carbs 4.06g; Fibre 0.5g; Sugar 2.55g; Protein 45.28g

Chapter 7 Dessert Recipes

Brownies with Peanuts

Prep time: 10 minutes | Cook time: 16 minutes | Serves: 8

105g brown sugar
65g peanut butter
3 tablespoons butter, melted
1 large egg
1 teaspoon vanilla

40g plain flour
⅛ teaspoon baking powder
Pinch sea salt
Nonstick baking spray containing flour
3 tablespoons chopped salted peanuts

1. In a medium bowl, combine the brown sugar, peanut butter, and butter and mix well. Add the egg and vanilla and beat to combine. 2. Stir in the flour, baking powder, and salt just until combined. 3. Spray a 15 cm round pan with the baking spray. Spread the batter into the pan. Sprinkle them with the peanuts. 4. Preheat the air fryer to 160°C on Air Fry mode. Place the pan in the air fryer basket and bake for 13 to 16 minutes or until the brownies look set and a toothpick inserted near the centre comes out with only a few moist crumbs. 5. Place the pan on a wire rack to cool. Cut the brownies into wedges to serve.

Per Serving: Calories 176; Fat 9.37g; Sodium 208mg; Carbs 20.89g; Fibre 0.8g; Sugar 15.48g; Protein 2.94g

Pistachio Pears

Prep time: 10 minutes | Cook time: 15 minutes | Serves: 4

2 large ripe pears (Bosc or Anjou)
2 tablespoons butter, melted
3 tablespoons brown sugar

⅛ teaspoon cinnamon
70g whole unsalted shelled pistachios
Pinch sea salt

1. Cut the pears in half lengthwise, leaving the stems on one half of each pear. Carefully remove the seeds using a melon baller or spoon. 2. Put the pears into the air fryer basket, cut-side up. Brush the pears with the melted butter, and then sprinkle with the brown sugar and cinnamon. 3. Preheat the air fryer to 175°C. Bake the pears for 8 minutes, then remove the basket from the air fryer. 4. Sprinkle the pears with the pistachios, concentrating them in the hollow where the seeds were. Sprinkle with the salt. 5. Return the basket to the air fryer. Bake for another 3 to 6 minutes or until the pears are tender and glazed. Serve.

Per Serving: Calories 164; Fat 12.89g; Sodium 102mg; Carbs 10.71g; Fibre 1.6g; Sugar 7.06g; Protein 3.3g

Apple & Berry Crumble

Prep time: 15 minutes | Cook time: 20 minutes | Serves: 4

1 large Granny Smith apple, peeled and chopped	75g brown sugar
75g chopped strawberries	55g butter, at room temperature
55g raspberries	30g plain flour
1 tablespoon freshly squeezed lemon juice	½ teaspoon cinnamon
2 tablespoons granulated sugar	Pinch sea salt
40g rolled oats	

1. In a 18cm round pan, combine the apple, strawberries, and raspberries. Drizzle with the lemon juice, then sprinkle with the sugar and toss to mix. 2. In a medium bowl, combine the oats, brown sugar, butter, flour, cinnamon, and salt and mix until crumbly, like coarse sand. 3. Sprinkle the oat mixture over the fruit in the pan. 4. Preheat the air fryer to 160°C on Air Fry mode. Put the pan in the air fryer basket. Bake the mixture for 15 to 20 minutes, checking after 15 minutes, until the fruit is bubbling and the topping is golden brown. Let cool for 20 minutes, and then serve.

Per Serving: Calories 300; Fat 12.61g; Sodium 98mg; Carbs 49.41g; Fibre 4.7g; Sugar 31.88g; Protein 3.53g

Jumbo Bar Cookie

Prep time: 15 minutes | Cook time: 18 minutes | Serves: 4

105g brown sugar	½ teaspoon baking powder
75g butter, at room temperature	¼ teaspoon sea salt
1 large egg	Nonstick baking spray containing flour
1 teaspoon vanilla	5 fun size chocolate, nut, and caramel bars
125g plain flour	

1. In a medium bowl, combine the brown sugar, butter, egg, and vanilla and mix well. 2. Add the flour, baking powder, and salt and mix just until a dough forms. 3. Spray a 18 cm round pan with the baking spray, line with parchment paper on the bottom, and spray the paper. 4. Divide the dough in half. Put half of the dough into the pan and spread out to the edges, patting gently. 5. Slice the candy bars into 1 cm pieces and put them on the dough in the pan, keeping them away from the edges. 6. Top the candy bar slices with the remaining dough and smooth out, being sure to cover all of the candy. Press down on the edges lightly to make sure the dough is sealed. 7. Set or preheat the air fryer to 175°C on Air Fry mode. Put the pan in the air fryer basket. Bake the food for 13 to 18 minutes, checking after 13 minutes, until the cookie is golden brown and set. 8. Carefully remove the pan and cool on a wire rack for 10 to 15 minutes before you attempt to remove the cookie. Serve whole. Let people break off pieces to eat.

Per Serving: Calories 370; Fat 16.63g; Sodium 277mg; Carbs 51.41g; Fibre 0.9g; Sugar 26.93g; Protein 4.1g

Tasty Pear Pecan Crostata

Prep time: 15 minutes | Cook time: 25 minutes | Serves: 4

2 ripe pears, peeled, cored, and chopped
70g coarsely chopped pecans
2 tablespoons granulated sugar

1 tablespoon plain flour
1 (12.5cm) round pie crust

1. In a medium bowl, combine the pears and pecans. Sprinkle with the sugar and flour and toss gently to coat. 2. Ease the pie crust into a 18cm spring-form pan. Press the crust down onto the bottom of the pan and up the sides. 3. Spoon the pear filling into the crust, spreading it evenly. 4. Gently pull the sides of the crust down over the filling, pleating the crust as you work, leaving the centre of the filling uncovered. 5. Preheat the air fryer to 175°C. Lower the spring-form pan into the basket in the air fryer. 6. Bake the food for 18 to 24 minutes or until the pears are tender and bubbling slightly, and the crust is light golden brown. 7. Remove the pan from the basket and let cool on a wire rack for about 20 minutes. Remove the sides of the pan and slice the crostata into wedges to serve.

Per Serving: Calories 363; Fat 24.25g; Sodium 292mg; Carbs 34.43g; Fibre 4.6g; Sugar 8.88g; Protein 4.71g

Gingerbread Crusted Nuts

Prep time: 15 minutes | Cook time: 15 minutes | Serves: 8 to 10

1 large egg white
Pinch sea salt
70g granulated sugar
75g brown sugar
½ teaspoon cinnamon

½ teaspoon ground ginger
⅛ teaspoon nutmeg
250g small whole pecans
2 tablespoons butter, melted

1. In a medium bowl, use a hand mixer to beat the egg white and salt until foamy. 2. Gradually beat in the granulated and brown sugars until the mixture starts to stiffen. Beat in the cinnamon, ginger, and nutmeg. 3. Fold the pecans into the meringue. 4. Line the air fryer basket with parchment paper. 5. Spread one-third of the nuts in an even layer in the basket and drizzle some butter on top. Repeat twice, making three layers of nuts and three layers of butter. 6. Preheat the air fryer to 150°C. Bake the food for 5 minutes, then remove basket and stir the nuts. Bake them for 5 minutes longer, and then stir again. Finally, bake for another 5 minutes or until the nuts are toasted and light brown. 7. Spread the nuts on a sheet of parchment paper and let stand for 1 hour. The nuts will be crisp. Store the dish in an airtight container at room temperature for up to 3 days.

Per Serving: Calories 234; Fat 20.14g; Sodium 41mg; Carbs 14.05g; Fibre 2.5g; Sugar 11.29g; Protein 2.68g

White Chocolate Blondies

Prep time: 15 minutes | Cook time: 20 minutes | Serves: 6

110g white chocolate chips	1 teaspoon vanilla
75g butter	125g plain flour
105g brown sugar	⅛ teaspoon sea salt
50g granulated sugar	Unsalted butter, at room temperature
1 large egg	55g semisweet chocolate chips
1 large egg yolk	

1. In a small saucepan over low heat, melt the white chocolate chips and butter for 4 to 5 minutes, stirring frequently until melted and combined. 2. Transfer the mixture to a medium bowl. Add the brown and granulated sugars and beat well. Then add the egg, egg yolk, and vanilla and beat until smooth. 3. Stir in the flour and salt until just combined. 4. Grease a spring-form pan with the unsalted butter. Cut out a piece of parchment paper to fit inside the pan and grease the paper. 5. Pour the batter into the pan and smooth the top. 6. Set or preheat the air fryer to 160°C. Place the pan in the air fryer basket. Bake the food for 15 to 20 minutes or until a toothpick inserted near the centre of the brownies comes out with only a few moist crumbs. 7. Remove the pan and let cool completely on a wire rack. 8. Melt the dark chocolate chips as directed on the package and drizzle on top.

Per Serving: Calories 419; Fat 20.78g; Sodium 158mg; Carbs 55.66g; Fibre 1.2g; Sugar 38.43g; Protein 4.69g

Bread Pudding with Dried Fruits

Prep time: 20 minutes | Cook time: 35 minutes | Serves: 4

180g whipping cream	1 teaspoon vanilla
120ml whole milk	Pinch sea salt
55g brown sugar	160g bread cubes
2 large egg yolks	30g dried cranberries
3 tablespoons butter, melted	35g golden raisins
2 tablespoons honey	Unsalted butter, at room temperature

1. Combine the cream, milk, brown sugar, egg yolks, butter, honey, vanilla, and salt in a large bowl. 2. Stir in the bread cubes. Stir in the cranberries and raisins. Let stand for 15 minutes. 3. Grease the bottom and sides of a 18 cm spring-form pan with the unsalted butter. Add the bread mixture. 4. Preheat the air fryer to 175°C. Put the pan in the air fryer basket. Bake them for 30 to 35 minutes or until the bread pudding is set and golden brown on top. 5. Remove from the air fryer and cool for 20 minutes, then serve.

Per Serving: Calories 429; Fat 21.39g; Sodium 311mg; Carbs 54.8g; Fibre 1.4g; Sugar 36.67g; Protein 6.3g

Chocolate Lava Cake with Raspberry

Prep time: 15 minutes | Cook time: 15 minutes | Serves: 4

50g semisweet chocolate chips
40g milk chocolate chips
55g butter
2 large eggs
1 large egg yolk
50g granulated sugar
3 tablespoons icing sugar
1 teaspoon vanilla

4 tablespoons plain flour
¼ teaspoon baking powder
Pinch sea salt
Unsalted butter, at room temperature
2 teaspoons cocoa powder
4 teaspoons raspberry jam
125g fresh raspberries
1 tablespoon freshly squeezed lemon juice

1. In a small microwave-safe bowl, melt the semisweet chocolate chips, milk chocolate chips, and butter in the microwave on medium power for 2 to 3 minutes. Remove and stir until combined and smooth, then set aside. 2. In a medium bowl, beat together the eggs and egg yolk. Gradually add the granulated and icing sugars, beating until the mixture is fluffy and lighter yellow in colour. Beat in the vanilla. 3. Add the flour, baking powder, and salt and mix until combined. Then fold in the chocolate and butter mixture. 4. Grease four 100 g glass heatproof ramekins with the unsalted butter. Sprinkle ½ teaspoon cocoa power in each ramekin and shake to coat. Shake out the excess cocoa powder. 5. Fill the ramekins half full with the batter. Top each with a teaspoon of the raspberry jam. Cover the jam with the rest of the batter. 6. Place the ramekins in the air fryer basket. You may be able to bake all four at one time, or just two at a time, depending on the size of your machine. 7. Preheat the air fryer to 190°C. Put the basket in the air fryer. Bake the food for 9 to 12 minutes or until the edges of the cake are set. 8. While the cakes are baking, place the raspberries and lemon juice in a small saucepan. Bring to a simmer over medium-low heat. Simmer for 2 to 4 minutes or until a sauce forms. Remove from heat and set aside. 9. Remove the basket from the air fryer and let the ramekins cool on a wire rack for 5 minutes. Run a knife around the edge of each ramekin and invert each cake onto a serving plate. Top with the sauce and serve.

Per Serving: Calories 368; Fat 19.63g; Sodium 112mg; Carbs 47g; Fibre 3.7g; Sugar 35.57g; Protein 4.81g

Berries Pavlova

Prep time: 10 minutes | Cook time: 45 minutes | Serves: 4

3 large egg whites	2 tablespoons icing sugar
Pinch sea salt	40g blueberries
140g granulated sugar	40g raspberries
1 teaspoon cornflour	40g chopped strawberries
1 teaspoon apple cider vinegar	1 teaspoon honey
120g whipping cream	

1. In a very clean mixing bowl, use a hand mixer to beat the egg whites and salt. 2. When soft peaks start to form, beat in the granulated sugar, one tablespoon at a time. Keep beating until the meringue is glossy and forms stiff peaks when the beater is lifted. 3. Fold in the cornflour and vinegar. 4. Cut a piece of parchment paper the same size as the bottom of a 18cm round pan. Put a dot of the meringue mixture on the bottom of the pan and add the parchment paper; this helps the paper stay in place. 5. Put the meringue mixture on the parchment paper, forming it into a disc and flattening the top and sides with a spatula. 6. Preheat the air fryer to 150°C. Place the pan in the air fryer basket and the basket in the air fryer and bake for 40 to 45 minutes or until the meringue is dry to the touch. Turn off the air fryer, pull the basket out about an inch, and let the meringue cool for 1 hour. 7. Remove the meringue from the air fryer and cool completely on a wire rack. 8. In a small bowl, beat the cream with the icing sugar until soft peaks form. 9. Turn the meringue over so the bottom is on top. Spread the cream over the meringue, then top with the blueberries, raspberries, and strawberries and drizzle with the honey.
Per Serving: Calories 195; Fat 5.72g; Sodium 88mg; Carbs 33.9g; Fibre 1.3g; Sugar 31.49g; Protein 3.4g

Mini Peanut Butter Cheesecake

Prep time: 10 minutes | Cook time: 10 minutes | Serves: 2

100g cream cheese, softened	butter
2 tablespoons erythritol	½ teaspoon vanilla extract
1 tablespoon all-natural, no-sugar-added peanut	1 large egg, whisked

1. In a medium bowl, mix cream cheese and erythritol until smooth. Add peanut butter and vanilla, mixing until smooth. Add egg and stir just until combined. 2. Spoon the mixture into an ungreased 10 cm spring-form nonstick pan and place into air fryer basket. 3. Air-fry the mixture at 150°C for 10 minutes until the edges are firm, but centre will be mostly set with only a small amount of jiggle when done. 4. Let pan cool at room temperature 30 minutes, cover with plastic wrap, then place into refrigerator at least 2 hours. Serve chilled.
Per Serving: Calories 223; Fat 20.71g; Sodium 252mg; Carbs 3.16g; Fibre 0.4g; Sugar 2.38g; Protein 6.55g

Butter Gingerbread

Prep time: 15 minutes | Cook time: 27 minutes | Serves: 6

125g plain flour	⅛ teaspoon ground cardamom
1 teaspoon ground ginger	75g brown sugar
½ teaspoon cinnamon	110g honey
½ teaspoon baking soda	80ml milk
¼ teaspoon sea salt	1 large egg yolk
⅛ teaspoon nutmeg	Unsalted butter, at room temperature

1. In a medium bowl, combine the flour, ginger, cinnamon, baking soda, salt, nutmeg, and cardamom and mix well. 2. In another medium bowl, combine the brown sugar, honey, milk, and egg yolk and beat until combined. 3. Stir the honey mixture into the flour mixture just until combined. 4. Grease a suitable round pan with the unsalted butter. Cut a piece of parchment paper to fit the bottom of the pan, and grease that. Pour in the batter. Cover the pan tightly with aluminum foil and poke a few holes in the foil with the tip of a knife. 5. Preheat the air fryer to 160°C. Put the pan in the air fryer basket. Bake the food for 22 to 27 minutes or until a toothpick inserted near the centre of the gingerbread comes out with only a few moist crumbs. 6. Remove from the air fryer and cool on a wire rack for 20 minutes, then cut into wedges to serve.

Per Serving: Calories 198; Fat 1.43g; Sodium 214mg; Carbs 44.33g; Fibre 0.8g; Sugar 27.82g; Protein 3.14g

Cream Puffs

Prep time: 15 minutes | Cook time: 25 minutes | Serves: 6

60g raspberries	55g butter
30g chopped strawberries	65g plain flour
30g blueberries	Pinch sea salt
1 tablespoon honey	2 large eggs
6 tablespoons water	

1. Combine the raspberries, strawberries, and blueberries with the honey in a small bowl and mix gently, set aside. 2. Combine the water and butter in a medium saucepan over high heat and bring to a rolling boil. Reduce the heat to medium and add the flour and salt. Beat well until the dough forms a ball and pulls away from the sides of the pan. 3. Remove the pan from the heat. Beat in the eggs, one at a time, until the dough is smooth and shiny. 4. Line a round cookie sheet with parchment paper. Working in batches, spoon three rounded tablespoons of the dough onto the cookie sheet (half the dough), 2.5cm apart. 5. Set or preheat the air fryer to 205°C. Put the cookie sheet in the air fryer basket. Bake the food for 18 to 24 minutes or until the cream puffs are puffed and golden brown. Remove the cream puffs and let cool on a wire rack. Repeat with remaining dough. 6. Slice the cream puffs in half crosswise. Remove any loose strands of dough, and fill with the fruit.

Per Serving: Calories 165; Fat 9.36g; Sodium 91mg; Carbs 18.84g; Fibre 1.3g; Sugar 9.7g; Protein 2.35g

Peppermint Bonbon Alaska

Prep time: 25 minutes | Cook time: 20 minutes | Serves: 4

50g plus 70g granulated sugar, divided	65g plain flour
55g butter, melted	20g cocoa powder
55g brown sugar	Pinch sea salt
2 large eggs, yolks and whites separated	Unsalted butter, at room temperature
1 teaspoon vanilla	480ml mint ice cream with chocolate chips

1. In a medium bowl, combine 50g of granulated sugar, the butter, and brown sugar and mix well. Beat in the egg yolks and vanilla. 2. Add the flour, cocoa powder, and salt and mix just until combined. Cover and refrigerate the egg whites. 3. Grease a round pan with the unsalted butter. Cut a piece of parchment paper to fit the bottom of the pan and grease it. Pour the brownie batter into the pan. Cover the pan with aluminum foil, crimping the edges to secure. Poke a few holes in the foil with the tip of a knife. 4. Preheat the air fryer to 160°C. Put the pan in the air fryer basket. Bake the food for 12 to 17 minutes or until a toothpick inserted near the centre comes out with only a few moist crumbs. 5. Remove the pan from the air fryer and cool for 20 minutes on a wire rack, then run a knife around the edges of the pan and invert the brownie onto the rack. Cool completely. 6. Line a 5-inch bowl with plastic wrap. Add the ice cream, pressing to fit the bowl. Smooth the flat surface of the ice cream. 7. Put the brownie on a 18cm round cookie sheet or in a -spring-form pan. 8. Invert the bowl onto the centre of the brownie, pressing down gently so the ice cream adheres to the brownie. Leave the plastic wrap around the ice cream. Cover the ice cream and brownie and freeze for at least 3 hours. 9. While the ice cream and brownie freeze, make the meringue. In a very clean medium bowl, beat the cold egg whites until frothy. Gradually add the remaining sugar, beating until stiff peaks form. 10. Remove the brownie and ice cream from the freezer. Remove the plastic. Carefully "frost" the whole thing with the meringue, just barely covering the brownie part, but frosting the ice cream thickly. Make swirls with your knife. 11. Freeze again, uncovered, for at least 3 hours. When it's frozen solid, you can carefully cover it with plastic wrap. Remove the plastic before baking. 12. When you're ready to eat, set or preheat the air fryer to 205°C. Lower the cookie sheet or pan into the air fryer basket using a foil sling or plate gripper. Bake them for 2 to 3 minutes or until the meringue is golden brown in spots. Carefully lift the dessert out of the air fryer using tongs to grip the foil sling or using the plate gripper. 13. Cut into fourths and serve immediately.

Per Serving: Calories 344; Fat 17.04g; Sodium 162mg; Carbs 44.88g; Fibre 2.2g; Sugar 28.41g; Protein 5.67g

Bread Rolls

Prep time: 1 hour 45 minutes | Cook time: 16 minutes | Serves: 5-6

375g flour, plus additional for dusting	240ml whole milk
120g bread flour	55g butter
3 teaspoons instant dry yeast	2 large eggs
1 tablespoon granulated sugar	Vegetable oil
½ teaspoon sea salt	

1. In a large bowl, combine the plain and bread flours. Stir in the yeast, sugar, and salt. 2. In a medium saucepan over low heat, combine the milk and butter. Heat for 4 to 6 minutes until the butter melts. 3. Combine the milk mixture with the flour mixture. Add the eggs and beat well. Keep stirring until a dough forms. 4. Lightly dust a work surface with plain flour. Turn the dough onto the work surface and knead with your hands until it is smooth, about 5 minutes. 5. Coat a large mixing bowl with the oil. Put the dough into the bowl. Turn the dough in the oil to coat it. Cover with a kitchen towel and let rise for 1 hour 30 minutes. It should double in volume. 6. Punch down the dough, and then divide into three parts if making rolls, or two parts if making pizza. Put each part into its own freezer bag labeled with the date and name. Freeze for up to 2 months. 7. Thaw the dough in the refrigerator overnight and proceed with the recipe. 8. Divide a one-third portion of dough into 7 balls. Line the air fryer basket with parchment paper and add the dough balls in a single layer. Cover the basket with a kitchen towel and let rise for 45 minutes. 9. Preheat the air fryer to 160°C. Bake the dough balls for 12 to 16 minutes or until the rolls are light golden brown. Let them cool on wire racks. 10. Cut out a round of parchment paper that fits into the air fryer basket. Roll out one half of the dough directly onto the round of paper. Place round in the basket. Top pizza dough as desired. 11. Preheat the air fryer to 205°C. Bake the food for 7 to 10 minutes or until the crust is crisp and the toppings are hot. Remove from the air fryer and place on a wire rack. Repeat with second half of dough.

Per Serving: Calories 453; Fat 13.67g; Sodium 367mg; Carbs 69.83g; Fibre 2.9g; Sugar 8.47g; Protein 11.96g

Pie Crust

Prep time: 20 minutes | Cook time: 10 minutes | Serves: 12

375g plain flour	60ml water
½ teaspoon sea salt	60ml milk
205g solid vegetable shortening	1 teaspoon freshly squeezed lemon juice
75g butter, cold	

1. Combine the flour and salt in a large bowl. 2. Cut in the shortening and butter. This means you work the fats into the flour until the shortening and butter are the size of small peas. 3. In a small bowl or measuring cup, combine the water, milk, and lemon juice. Drizzle the liquid ingredients over the flour and fat mixture and combine with a fork, until the dough starts to come together. 4. Work the mixture until a dough forms. You may need to add a bit more water if the dough seems dry. 5. Divide the dough into thirds to make pie crusts that fit a round pan. You can freeze the dough for up to 2 months. To thaw, let stand at room temperature for an hour or two until it's workable. 6. Roll out one portion of dough between two sheets of waxed paper to form a 25cm round circle. Use as directed in the recipe. 7. Preheat the air fryer to 175°C. Put the pie plate in the air fryer basket. Bake the pie for 8 to 10 minutes or until the crust is light golden brown and set. Let cool on a rack and fill with custard, ice cream, or fresh fruit.

Per Serving: Calories 313 Fat 22.61g; Sodium 141mg; Carbs 24.12g; Fibre 0.8g; Sugar 0.36g; Protein 3.44g

Chocolate Doughnuts

Prep time: 10 minutes | Cook time: 10 minutes | Serves: 10

100g blanched finely ground almond flour	½ teaspoon baking powder
20g low-carb vanilla protein powder	2 large eggs, whisked
20g granular erythritol	½ teaspoon vanilla extract
20g unsweetened cocoa powder	

1. Mix all ingredients in a large bowl until a soft dough forms. Separate and roll dough into twenty balls, about 2 tablespoons each. 2. Cut a piece of parchment to fit your air fryer basket. Working in batches if needed, place doughnut holes into air fryer basket on ungreased parchment. 3. Air-fry the doughnut holes at 195°C for 6 minutes, flipping doughnut holes halfway through cooking. Doughnut holes will be golden and firm when done. 4. Let the dish cool for 10 minutes before serving.

Per Serving: Calories 152; Fat 11.39g; Sodium 198mg; Carbs 6.22g; Fibre 2.5g; Sugar 1.63g; Protein 9.42g

Brown Sugar Cookies

Prep time: 5 minutes | Cook time: 30 minutes | Serves: 4

4 tablespoons salted butter, melted	½ teaspoon vanilla extract
60g granular brown erythritol	100g blanched finely ground almond flour
1 large egg	½ teaspoon baking powder

1. In a large bowl, whisk together butter, erythritol, egg, and vanilla. Add flour and baking powder, and stir until combined. 2. Separate dough into nine pieces and roll into balls, about 2 tablespoons each. 3. Cut three pieces of parchment paper to fit your air fryer basket and place three cookies on each ungreased piece. Place one piece of parchment into air fryer basket. 4. Bake the food at 150°C for 9 minutes. Edges of cookies will be browned when done. Do the same with the remaining cookies. 5. Serve warm.

Per Serving: Calories 353; Fat 31.57g; Sodium 388mg; Carbs 8.13g; Fibre 3.6g; Sugar 1.77g; Protein 13.71g

Simple Cake

Prep time: 10 minutes | Cook time: 30 minutes | Serves: 8

200g blanched finely ground almond flour	60g granular erythritol
5 large eggs, whisked	1 teaspoon vanilla extract
180ml extra-virgin olive oil	1 teaspoon baking powder

1. Mix all ingredients in a large bowl. Pour batter into an ungreased 15 cm round nonstick baking dish. 2. Place dish into air fryer basket. Bake the food at 150°C for 30 minutes. 3. The cake will be golden on top and firm in the centre when done. 4. Let cake cool in dish 30 minutes before slicing and serving.

Per Serving: Calories 357; Fat 32.45g; Sodium 345mg; Carbs 7.93g; Fibre 3.6g; Sugar 1.8g; Protein 12.12g

Chocolate Chip Cookie

Prep time: 5 minutes | Cook time: 15 minutes | Serves: 8

4 tablespoons salted butter, melted	100g blanched finely ground almond flour
60g granular brown erythritol	½ teaspoon baking powder
1 large egg	40g chocolate chips
½ teaspoon vanilla extract	

1. In a large bowl, whisk together butter, erythritol, egg, and vanilla. Add flour and baking powder, and stir until combined. 2. Fold in chocolate chips, and then spoon batter into an ungreased 15cm round nonstick baking dish. 3. Place dish into air fryer basket. Bake the batter at 150°C for 15 minutes until the edges are browned. 4. Slice and serve warm.

Per Serving: Calories 176; Fat 15.79g; Sodium 194mg; Carbs 4.07g; Fibre 1.8g; Sugar 0.89g; Protein 6.85g

Chilled Strawberry Pie

Prep time: 15 minutes | Cook time: 10 minutes | Serves: 6

165g whole shelled pecans
1 tablespoon unsalted butter, softened
240g heavy whipping cream

12 medium fresh strawberries, hulled
2 tablespoons sour cream

1. Place pecans and butter into a food processor and pulse ten times until a dough forms. Press dough into the bottom of an ungreased 15cm round nonstick baking dish. 2. Place dish into air fryer basket. Bake the pie at 160°C for 10 minutes. Crust will be firm and golden when done. Let cool 20 minutes. 3. In a large bowl, whisk cream for 2 minutes until fluffy and doubled in size. 4. In a separate large bowl, mash strawberries until mostly liquid. Fold strawberries and sour cream into whipped cream. 5. Spoon the mixture into cooled crust, cover, and place into refrigerator for at least 30 minutes to set. Serve chilled.

Per Serving: Calories 265; Fat 26.99g; Sodium 12mg; Carbs 6.12g; Fibre 2.9g; Sugar 2.72g; Protein 3.06g

Chocolate Soufflés

Prep time: 5 minutes | Cook time: 15 minutes | Serves: 2

2 large eggs, whites and yolks separated
1 teaspoon vanilla extract

50g chocolate chips
2 teaspoons coconut oil, melted

1. In a medium bowl, beat egg whites until stiff peaks form, about 2 minutes. Set aside. In a separate medium bowl, whisk egg yolks and vanilla together. Set aside. 2. In a separate medium microwave-safe bowl, place chocolate chips and drizzle with coconut oil. Microwave on high 20 seconds, then stir and continue cooking in 10-second increments until melted, being careful not to overheat chocolate. Let them cool 1 minute. 3. Slowly pour melted chocolate into egg yolks and whisk until smooth. Then, slowly begin adding egg white mixture to chocolate mixture, about ¼ cup at a time, folding in gently. 4. Pour the mixture into two 10 cm ramekins greased with cooking spray. Place ramekins into air fryer basket. 5. Air-fry the food at 205°C for 15 minutes. 6. Soufflés will puff up while cooking and deflate a little once cooled. The centre will be set when done. Let cool 10 minutes, then serve warm.

Per Serving: Calories 167; Fat 12.61g; Sodium 30mg; Carbs 8.47g; Fibre 1.4g; Sugar 2.16g; Protein 3.77g

Conclusion

You can prepare all of your meals for the day in one location using an air fryer. If you own an air fryer, use the wide variety of recipes presented in this cookbook. Your air fryer may be used to make anything, including wholesome lunches, snacks, dinners, and desserts. Here comes a comprehensive air fryer recipe cookbook that has exciting and amazing ideas to enjoy the same old food but with lesser oil and fewer calories. Each recipe comes with broad, simple-to-follow directions that work with any air fryer. Since each air fryer has its own control panel with particular features, you must use the temperature and time settings of the recipes in accordance with the user manual that comes with your appliance.

A

Apple & Berry Crumble   91
Apple-Cinnamon Cookies   23
Apricot Chicken   66
Asian Fish   74
Avocado Rice Bowls   34
Avocado Tacos   30

B

Balsamic Marinated Rib Eye Steak   80
Barbecue Chicken Drumsticks   52
Barbecue Pulled Jackfruit   26
Barbecued Back Ribs   87
Beef & Broccoli   83
Beef Cheese Empanadas   85
Beef Lettuce Wraps   84
Beef Spinach Braciole   81
Berbere-Spiced Potato Fries   47
Berries Pavlova   95
Bread Pudding with Dried Fruits   93
Bread Rolls   98
Bread-crumbed Fish   72
Breaded Chicken Breasts   64
Breaded Salmon with Cheese   76
Breaded White Mushrooms   32
Broccoli Salad   25
Broccoli Salad   28
Broiled Tilapia Fillets   71
Brown Sugar Cookies   100
Brownies with Peanuts   90
Butter Gingerbread   96

C

Cajun Prawns   75
Cajun Salmon   76
Calamari Tubes   74
Cauliflower Pizza Crust   37
Cauliflower Steak   30
Cheddar Spinach Omelet   14
Cheese Bean Taquitos   26
Cheese Courgette Boats   34
Cheese Pepper Eggs   14
Cheese Soufflés   15
Cheese Tilapia Fillets   72
Cheese Vegetarian Lasagna   33
Cheese Zoodle   36
Chicken Drumsticks with Sweet Rub   65
Chicken Fajitas & Street Corn   55
Chicken Fajitas   59
Chicken Parmesan   64
Chicken Steak   89
Chicken Tenders with Parmesan   53

Chicken with Broccoli   58
Chicken with Pineapple Cauliflower Rice   56
Chicken with Potato Salad   61
Chicken with Roasted Snap Peas   57
Chili Dogs   27
Chilled Strawberry Pie   101
Chocolate Chip Cookie   100
Chocolate Chip Muffins   11
Chocolate Doughnuts   99
Chocolate Lava Cake with Raspberry   94
Chocolate Soufflés   101
Chopped Blueberry Muffins   13
Chunky Canned Fish   73
Cinnamon Pecan Granola   17
Coconut Chicken Tenders   59
Cod   69
Courgette Sticks   39
Crab Croquettes   70
Cranberry Burgers   83
Cream Puffs   96
Cream Salmon   73
Crispy Butter Chicken   63
Crispy Prawns   55
Crispy Tofu & Sweet Potato   25
Crust Salmon   75
Crusted Chicken   61
Curry Samosa Rolls   22
Cute Bagels   12

D

Dill Chicken Strips   66

E

Easy Chicken Thighs   60
Easy-to-Cook Asparagus   49

F

Fast-Cooked Courgette Rolls   49
Fish Fillet   68
Fish Fingers   68
Flank Steak with Peppers   78
Fluffy Bacon Quiche   15
French Fries with Shallots   46
French Whole-Grain Toast   19
Fried Green Tomatoes   41
Fried Turkey Breast   65
Fried Turkey Wings   51
Fruit Muffins   18

G

Garlic Chicken Pizza   52
Garlic Russet Potatoes   43
Garlic Tortilla Chips   41
Gingerbread Crusted Nuts   92

Glazed Apple Fritters   23
Glazed Brussels Sprouts   47
Glazed Carrots   40
Glory Muffins   24
Goat Cheese–Stuffed Chicken Breast   67
Golden Pancake   24
Greek Lamb Burgers   88
Grilled Chicken Breasts   56

H

Halibut Steak   70
Ham Eggs   13
Homemade Giant Nachos   29
Homemade Hash Browns   20
Honey Mustard Ham   77

I

Indian Okra   48

J

Jalapeño & Bacon Pizza   17
Jerk-Flavoured Pork Loin   89
Jumbo Bar Cookie   91
Jumbo Prawns   71

K

Kale Chips   45

L

Lemon Aubergine Dip   31
Lemon Fish Fillets   69
Lemon Pork Tenderloin   87
Lemon-Pepper Chicken Thighs   51
Low-Fat Buffalo Cauliflower   42

M

Maple-Mustard Glazed Turkey Tenderloin   62
Marinated Tofu Cubes   27
Meatballs inTomato Sauce   86
Mini Mushroom-Onion Pizzas   31
Mini Peanut Butter Cheesecake   95
Mini Portobello Pizzas   38

O

Oat Bowls   19
Onion Avocado Bagels   22
Onion Rings   43
Onion Salmon Patties   71

P

Pakoras   45
Panko Boneless Pork Chops   86
Parmesan Courgette Chips   50
Parmesan Tilapia   75
Pecan-Crusted Chicken   67
Peppermint Bonbon Alaska   97
Pie Crust   99
Pineapple Salsa   33
Pistachio Pears   90
Pork Chops   79
Pork Teriyaki   88
Potato-Stuffed Peppers   29
Power Tarts   21

Prawns & Bacon Slices   73

Q

Quinoa Patties   32
Quinoa Quiche   18

R

Ranch Turkey Tenders with Vegetable Salad   62
Rib Eye Cheesesteaks   82
Roast Beef with Potatoes   82
Roasted Lemon Cauliflower   37
Roasted Shishito Peppers   44

S

Salmon Croquettes with Parsley   72
Salmon Fillets   76
"Samosas" with Coriander Chutney   44
Sausage Meatballs   16
Savory Egg Pizza   17
Savoury Potato Wedges   50
Seasoned Sweet Potato Wedges   50
Simple Cake   100
Simple Courgette   39
Simple French Fries   46
Simple Muffins   13
Southern Fried Chicken   63
Special Patties   21
Spicy Chicken Sandwiches   60
Spicy Chicken Wings   54
Spicy Grilled Steak   80
Spinach & Artichoke Casserole   36
Spring Rolls   48
Steak Fajitas   79
Stuffed Aubergine   35
Stuffed Potatoes with Dressing   28
Super-Filling Calzones   11
Sweet Potato Chips   49

T

Taco Pizza   78
Tamari Aubergine   40
Tasty Pear Pecan Crostata   92
Tasty Sausage-Crusted Egg Cups   16
T-bone Steak with Salsa   77
Tofu Scramble Brunch   20
Tomato Egg White Cups   14
Turkey Breast with Green Bean Casserole   53
Turkey Burgers   16
Turkey Meatloaf   54

V

Vanilla Cinnamon Rolls   12
Vanilla Pancakes   15
Vegan Sandwiches   26
Vegetable Quesadilla   35
Veggie Bowl   38

W

White Chocolate Blondies   93

Y

Yummy Jalapeño Egg Cups   19

Printed in Great Britain
by Amazon